Pulling Leather

Reuben Baker Mullins in 1885, after one year on the Wyoming range. *Photo courtesy Priscilla Hogan.*

Pulling Leather

Being the Early Recollections of a Cowboy on the Wyoming Range, 1884–1889

by
Reuben B. Mullins

Edited & with Introduction by

Jan Roush
Utah State University

Lawrence Clayton
Hardin-Simmons University

HIGH PLAINS PRESS
Glendo, Wyoming

Cover:
"Pullin' leather shows a heap of sense."
Wyoming State Archives, Museums and Historical Department

Library of Congress Cataloging-in Publication Data

Mullins, Reuben B., 1863–1935.
Pulling leather: being the early recollections of a cowboy on the Wyoming Range, 1884–1889.

Includes biography and index.   .
1. Mullins, Reuben B., 1863–1935. 2. Cowboys—Wyoming—Biography. 3. Frontier and pioneer life—Wyoming. 4. Wyoming—Social life and customs.
I. Roush, Jan. II. Clayton, Lawrence. III. Title.
F761.M85   1988   987.7'02'0924—dc19   88-16491
ISBN 0-931271-10-X (pbk.)

To the indomitable spirit of the frontier
found in the old-time Wyoming cowboy
and to this continuing tradition
alive today in both cowboys and buckaroos.

Introduction xi
I Worked on the Sybille Ditch 1
Blacksmithing at Chugwater 10
A Cowboy for a Day 18
With the AU7 Outfit 24
A Cowboy Welcome 34
A Period of Depression 40
Working the Town Herd 47
A Hot Footrace 53
A Slow Race 59
My First General Roundup 65
One Tough Drive 72
Two Kinds of Rustlers 77
Making Hay 83
Our Relations with Indians 88
Trailing a Beef Herd 94
Never Again 101
That Kangaroo Court 108
Lost in a Wyoming Blizzard 114
Experiencing a Calamity 120
Indians Raid the Ranch 125
Depression Everywhere 130

BREAKING BRONCOS 136
BADLY PUNCTURED 141
A TOUGH DEAL 147
A SIX-SHOOTER EPISODE 154
REPRESENTING 159
IN CLOVER 165
NEW FRIENDS 171
SALT CREEK 175
FIGHTING A PRAIRIE FIRE 182
A MAN WITH A TEMPER 187
THE OPEN RANGE DOOMED 190
Appendix A: Letters from Friends 197
Appendix B: About the Author 203
Further Reading 212
Index 214

LIST OF ILLUSTRATIONS

Reuben Baker Mullins in 1885	ii
Map, Wyoming 1887	xxiv
Cheyenne-Deadwood Stage	14
Cowboys on Powder River	62
Reuben Mullins on the AU7	168
Dr. Reuben Mullins in 1905	193

ABOUT THE EDITORS

JAN ELIZABETH ROUSH is on the English Faculty at Utah State University at Logan, Utah, where she is Director of the Writing Center. She holds the doctorate in English from East Texas State University in Commerce. Her interests include cowboy poetry as a reflection of the life of the old-time and modern cowboy as well as theories of literary criticism and rhetoric.

LAWRENCE CLAYTON is Dean of the College of Arts & Sciences and a professor of English at Hardin-Simmons University in Abilene, Texas. He holds the doctorate from Texas Tech University in Lubbock, Texas. His research interests include life and literature of the West, especially songs of the old-time cowboys and contemporary cowboy life in Texas.

ACKNOWLEDGEMENTS

We wish to express our appreciation first of all for the help of A. J. Simmonds, Head, Special Collections Archive, Utah State University, where this manuscript was originally discovered. Simmonds also provided valuable assistance in locating supporting materials, photographs, and historical data. Ruby Preuit and the late Agnes Wright Spring graciously shared their knowledge of Wyoming history and assisted in our search for background material.

Our thanks go to the Wyoming State Archives and Historical Department for prompt attention to our requests for information and to Paula McDougal, photo archivist, University of Wyoming American Heritage Center, for her extensive photo searches.

Special thanks also go to Joy Cron of Hardin-Simmons University whose proficient word processing skills provided successive drafts of clean copy and helped shape the final manuscript.

Finally, we owe a large debt to Nancy Curtis of High Plains Press, first for locating the unedited version of Mullins' text in the Wyoming State Archives, but, most importantly, for her indefatigable encouragement and support during work on the project.

Introduction

THE MANUSCRIPT WHICH follows is interesting on two levels: what it says and how it came to light. It is interesting in itself since it offers a remarkably fluent and lucid firsthand account of an important and exciting era in the settlement of the West: the early days of the cattle industry. Using Wyoming as its backdrop, the manuscript specifically chronicles those years just prior to statehood when empires based on cattle were the primary force in settling the Wyoming Territory. The time period covered in this narrative is five years, five significant years ranging from 1884 to 1889 during which time the cattle industry in Wyoming rose to its peak and then plunged into disaster in the wake of the devastating blizzard in the winter of 1885–86.

The author, Reuben Baker Mullins, is a literate man with a philosophical bent who has lent his well-developed powers of perception to recording the events he either participated in or observed during the time he cowboyed; that in itself is unique, placing his narrative in the august company of such other literate and perceptive accounts of cowboy life as Teddie "Blue" Abbott's *We Pointed Them North*, Charles Siringo's *A Texas Cowboy*, and Andy Adams' *Log of a Cowboy*. Even more significant is that Mullins writes this account from the perspective of almost fifty years, which allows him to look back on this life and comment also on its historical significance. This distance is what enables him to note especially

the romanticizing elements which have crept into describing
such a life, quite in contrast to its harsh reality. From time
to time he comments wryly on this discrepancy.

How this manuscript came to light is a composite of co-
incidental events fifty-five years in the making. After cowboying for five years, Reuben B. Mullins went on to become
a doctor and then a dentist, practicing first in Broken Bow
and other small towns in Nebraska before finally settling in
Fremont. In the 1930s, toward the end of his long, professional life, Dr. Mullins decided to record the experiences of
his younger years—for his family, but also because he realized
the historical significance of these experiences. For this manuscript he wrote a preface in which he details his purpose:

> *Lest we forget the departed Cowboy, and the open
> range, it would seem fitting that a description should be
> given by one who still lives that participated in the cattle
> business during the eighties when it was at its peak. In
> doing so, I have set down my own personal experiences
> while riding the range during those far-away days, while
> nothing but facts have been recorded in this narrative.*
>
> *Many writers of fiction portray this wild and ro-
> mantic life of cowboys, yet through the years of my
> experience while engaged in the actual work, the romance
> supposed to be a part of such a life failed to show up.
> However, I did find such a life and work a continual
> round of drudgery, exposure, and hard work which begger
> description, and in no case is the departed cowboy de-
> serving of the obituary given him by commercialized
> writers.*
>
> *I have in my story tried to give a comprehensive
> routine of cowboy life and work, just as it was conducted
> through all its diversified ramifications, which were
> manifold.*

Mullins' efforts to secure a publisher were futile; unfortunately, he died of a cerebral hemorrhage in 1935 before succeeding in his endeavors. The manuscript found a place only

in the files of Dr. Mullins' descendants. Later, probably around 1940, someone presented a copy of the document to the Wyoming State Historical Department; we assume that it was Dr. Mullins' son, Gifford. About this same time an unknown editor prepared a shortened version of the document, which was incorporated into a WPA Federal Writers Project focusing on the history of grazing in the western United States. As the work on the massive project approached its final stage under the editorship of George Willison, Pearl Harbor was bombed and the United States entered World War II, changing career plans and assignments of persons working on the project, which subsequently stalled and was abandoned. But the materials remained and were eventually transferred to the Special Collections Archive at Utah State University, where they lay largely unnoticed for a number of years.

In 1986 we discovered the shortened manuscript in Utah's Special Collections Archive and recognized it as a unique contribution to the history of this often-romanticized period in the development of the United States, though a contribution which, because of these unusual circumstances, had been ignored for over half a century. Very few clues to the origin of the manuscript were available. The author's name appeared on the cover sheet, but it was accompanied by a note written by Agnes Wright Spring, then director of the Federal Writers Project in Wyoming, requesting that the author's name not appear on the publication. We located Mrs. Spring in Fort Collins, Colorado, and interviewed her concerning the narrative. Mrs. Spring recalled the piece and expressed regret that she had been unable to pursue publication of what she even then had recognized as a valuable contribution to history, but she could offer no explanation for the notation; it had simply accompanied the submission of the manuscript. Who had requested the author's anonymity was never revealed, but one thing is certain: it was not Reuben Baker Mullins' request since we later were able to determine just how extensive his efforts had been to publish this narrative of his cowboying adventures.

Encouraged by Mrs. Spring's assessment of the manuscript, we redoubled our efforts to seek a publisher for it, contacting Nancy Curtis of High Plains Press, who also recognized the value of the document and agreed to publish it. It was her efforts which turned up the version of the narrative printed here, locating it among papers in the archive of the Wyoming State Historical Department where it had been divided into three sections, each filed separately.

In the meantime, in order to learn more about the manuscript, we searched for descendants of Dr. Mullins, an effort that led to the discovery of Gifford Mullins' widow in Lincoln, Nebraska. She in turn referred us to her daughter, Priscilla Hogan, who possessed many of her grandfather's papers. Mrs. Hogan kindly furnished many of the photographs used here, along with the details of her grandfather's personal life, a digest of which appears in the appendix "About the Author," and letters from such eminent Wyoming personalities as Harry Crain, James Dahlman, Duncan Grant, and John Kendrick, who both attest to the worth of Dr. Mullins' narrative and encourage his efforts to publish it.

Once we had in our possession the longer, unexpurgated version of the narrative and the information about the larger circumstances of Dr. Mullins' life from his descendants, we were able to present an account of this era of Wyoming history which we feel Dr. Mullins would approve. The manuscript for the most part remains as it was originally written, for Dr. Mullins had as keen a sense of style and perception about his life on the range as any which have been written. Our editing was confined for the most part to standardizing and sometimes modernizing the spelling and punctuation and occasionally combining some of the shorter paragraphs for greater fluency. Where appropriate we have added explanatory notes, which also contain references to sources giving further information. In the section "Further Reading," we have provided titles of other books which would provide additional information about cowboy life on the Wyoming range during the time of the narrative.

II

This manuscript contains basically the story of a young Wyoming cowboy whose adventures are characteristic of the time. Heeding the advice of Horace Greeley to "go West," the young Mullins first gets himself employed as a blacksmith on the Sybille Ditch, an irrigation project in southeastern Wyoming. He does not stay there long, however, for a lynching incident sours him on remaining. Packing up, he hikes the forty miles to Chugwater, where he catches the stage to Cheyenne. Back again in Cheyenne, Mullins decides to use his blacksmith trade as a means to land a job with a cow outfit. Reasoning that his skills would come in handy for shoeing horses, repairing branding irons, and fixing wagons and other equipment, he applies for work at the Swan Land and Cattle Company and is hired to work at the main ranch at Chugwater; here he quickly settles into his shop and wins the respect of all for his blacksmithing abilities. Especially impressed with Mullins' work is Duncan Grant, the assistant manager, who frequently pitches in and helps at the forge any time during the summer that he has a spare moment. Throughout the summer Mullins never loses the desire to do some actual cowboying, and as payment for a job well done, Grant arranges for Mullins to do just that when the fall roundup begins. In the process, he sets the stage for a classic re-enactment of the favorite frontier greenhorn trick.

One of the common tricks of the frontier was to put an unsuspecting greenhorn on the back of an outlaw bronc, and Duncan Grant does exactly that. Acceding to Reuben's wishes, he encourages the young would-be cowboy to get on a long-legged bay, which bucks his best but is unable to unseat the doughty young man. Grabbing the saddle horn with both hands in a death grip, Mullins manages to stay on, riding an outlaw bronc that many seasoned cowpunchers had been unable to. By "pulling leather" he survives the wild ride and manages to subdue the bronc, beginning a five-year period which chronicles his growth into an experienced top hand.

Later in the day Grant puts the young man on what would today be called a cutting horse, which provides another challenge for the aspiring cowboy. Again Mullins surprises the seasoned veterans by handling the task with aplomb. Even though his muscles are painfully sore from the experience, he is hooked on the life. After this one day with the cowboys, he returns to his forge until the end of the season and then leaves Wyoming for the winter, as was common practice. Returning to Iowa he puts in some time at the What Cheer mine, a trade he sometimes followed during those months that the weather prohibited working with cattle.

His dream of cowboying, however, did not die. Undaunted, Mullins returns the next spring and gets a job as a cowboy on the AU7 Ranch, a cattle spread that still exists in the same area where it was established about 1880. He works there for three years, learning his trade and developing into a top hand. Consistently given a poor string of horses and assigned some tasks that he considers unnecessarily dangerous, he leaves the AU7 at the end of his third season, determined that he will not work for that ranch again. When he returns there the next spring, the hands expect him to stay, but he rides on to the neighboring 4W Ranch, where he hires on and draws the wages of a top hand. Eventually Mullins works his way up to being a "rep," a representative of the ranch at roundups on neighboring ranges, finally emerging as one of the well-respected members of a class of people that he had long admired.

During his adventures, Mullins is exposed to many demanding situations: the vigilante hanging of a young man who had killed a friend in a drunken rage, an Indian burial ground in which the bodies were lashed in the tops of trees, a coal mine that had somehow caught on fire and had continued to burn for years, a prairie fire, a cursing granger boss, and a raging river at flood stage. He also participated in many of the joys of the frontier; as a member of a group of young cowboys whom he considered the finest collection of young men in America, he took part in boxing matches, footraces, and home ranch rodeos. He slept through shortened summer nights on the open range in his soogan to be roused by the cook's calls of "chuck" and rose to a hearty breakfast prepared in Dutch ovens. He met some of the best and worst horses that the Western rangelands had to offer, riding through life-threatening snowstorms and taking many other chances. Mullins demonstrates in his narrative a penchant for aesthetics, for he is willing to ride miles on horseback while his companions are napping in order to observe the beauty of the Belle Fourche plain. Even though his friend, Sam, warns him that the act is a dangerous one, Mullins goes anyway and views a scene he is still able to recall vividly many years later. No shy, retiring lad is Mullins. He faces life directly and wrests a full measure from it. After numerous such adventures, however, the veteran cowboy decides he has had enough of the range, sells his cowboy gear, and goes on to other interests in life.

In authenticity and perception, this document ranks among the best. Mullins may be less expansive than some documenters of the nomadic cowboy who herded the longhorns on the open range and drove them along the grueling trails to market; yet the very succinctness of the document in itself underscores the loneliness and the hardships that comprised such a life, quite in contrast to the usual Hollywood interpretation. Indeed, the author pauses periodically to ironically note this very contrast.

He is able to note that contrast more, perhaps, than most because the almost fifty years between the actual experience and his relating of it have given this former cowboy the objectivity to see in retrospect what writers and film makers have done to the real cowboy, and he does not like it. This veteran of the range is disgusted by the Hollywood version of the West and frequently notes in his account the contrast between the real and the fictional. Having spent several years of his life cowboying under frequently adverse conditions, he knows that glamour plays a minor role. The cowboys he worked with were doing a dirty, demanding job—and doing it well—and he is repulsed by the misrepresentation of reality. He knows that these were not supermen he worked with; rather they were just ordinary men doing the job they were hired to do, ordinary men who helped open the Wyoming Territory for settlement, and their contribution deserves whatever credit can be generated for them. Mullins' narrative is a chronicle of that process of coping with frontier hardships in early eastern Wyoming.

The value of the narrative as a documentary of the life of the cowboy is high. The narrator relates how he learned to be a cowboy, an exciting but often dangerous undertaking. Many of the experiences the narrator relates, though they do not usually highlight these dangers, at least convey the idea that risk to limb, if not to life itself, is an ever-present reality of the range environment. As the narrative opens, Mullins watches "cowboys and would-be cowboys disgorge from . . . trains" in that historic Union Pacific station in Cheyenne, Wyoming, bent on becoming part of an exciting adventure— an open range cowboy. Interwoven with these adventures we see the workings of the culture: a kangaroo court dispensing frontier justice, a "rodeo" performed on the "town herd," the routine of repairing equipment in the blacksmith shop. We get a clear picture of the cowboy by riding with him on both general and ranch roundups, working stock on the range, collecting mavericks, culling the herd, and branding calves with a running iron. We learn how cattlemen coped with the increasing pressures of disappearing rangeland through the description of the Stock Growers Association and their practice of blacklisting uncooperative cowboys. We also get a sense of impending doom for the demise of such a life as the narrator chronicles the efforts of cowboys and ranchers to cope with the devastating winter of 1886 when cattle by the thousands perished in the storms, leaving the ranges and the streams choked with the rotting bodies of dead livestock.

Nor did the devastation end there. The changes in the range cattle industry begun by an act of nature were exacerbated by two additional factors: the coming of the railroad the next year and the introduction of sheep. The narrative conveys how both factors ultimately changed the open range. The first brought settlers who plowed the land and fenced the water sources, preventing the cattle from ranging freely in search of food and water. The second caused serious conflict between cattlemen and sheepmen that cost many lives and fomented hardship for both sides.

Hence the narrative becomes important in an historical sense because it is a firsthand account of the boom and bust of an era: the huge roundups and the range life associated with them followed by the demise of the longhorn cattle industry after the climatic and financial disasters of 1885–1887. The author vividly records, from a firsthand perspective, how such disasters affected the cattle industry, some feel so severely as to declare both the industry and the cowboy who was such an integral part of it a thing of the past. True, as the narrator notes, the range as it was then never regained quite the same character it had before such changes occurred, but that life did go on. It might have altered, but the men who have that same spirit follow the outlaw steer to this day in the mold of this plucky Westerner who sees from the perspective of a half century later that he was fortunate to have been part of a great movement that helped settle the West.

Other items included in the narrative provide interesting commentary from an historical perspective as well as shedding further light on the folk life of the times. Of particular historical signficance, for example, is the amount of emphasis given to an issue still under debate today: the cowboy's practice of singing when on night herd to ward off a possible stampede. Mullins confirms that a steer startled by the sudden appearance of a mounted cowboy was apt to run; the singing kept the animals aware of the men's presence. The narrative also provides some interesting commentary on the political climate of the day as the narrator discusses his political

awakening in time to join in with the "Cleveland Democrats."

Of historical interest, too, are the recreational activities
resorted to by the cowboys in their spare time, which the
narrator discusses fully. Describing such activities as boxing,
horse racing, bronc busting, and other, more passive, activities such as dominoes, checkers, cribbage, and reading, the
narrator allows us a front row seat in watching the cowboy
at play, an area not always treated so fully in other documents
of the time. We are allowed to look over the men's shoulders,
as it were, at their foodways, their social hierarchy, and their
personal relationships.

The omissions within the narrative are also important in
what they reveal about that particular era. For instance, there
are only veiled hints of the cowboys' relations with prosti-
tutes, probably stemming from a reluctance at the time to
address such topics. That female relationships were an important part of cowboy life, however, can be seen from the
number of different references made about women by the
author and his friends. The treatment of women in the manuscript is interesting, for it confirms what historical assess-
ments of cowboy relationships with women have said, namely,
that cowboys tended to classify women into two types: those
they put on a pedestal, such as mothers, sisters, and sweet-
hearts; and those they cavorted with on their rare visits to
town.

With the former category, cowboys had a difficult time
interacting because of the awe they had built up for these
women, an awe only intensified by the little opportunity they
had to mingle with those of the opposite sex except on rare
occasions of dances or other social gatherings. In this wild
country, women, even wives, were still a rarity. The narrator
cites an interesting incident which typifies this dilemma. A
married woman visits the ranch with her husband and joins
the entire group in the mess hall. The men are all tongue-
tied and the narrator most of all, for he finds himself seated

next to her, forced into some kind of conversational exchange. Says the narrator of the men as they entered the room, "Every puncher's jaws snapped together like steel traps, and they wouldn't open their mouths except for the reception of food." The men were too afraid of saying something they should not. After two such miserable meals, the wife travels on with her husband, leaving behind some very relieved cowboys.

Though they did not always know how to handle interactions with women, the cowboys did desire female contact to help alleviate the loneliness of their lives. One of the most humorous incidents captured in this narrative involves their efforts to establish mail-order romances. How they go about this and what twists of fate result forms one of the funniest, yet most revealing, vignettes of cowboy life. The face-to-face meeting with the young woman with whom the narrator had corresponded makes for an interesting evening for him and a good story for his friends back in Wyoming when he later recounts it in the bunkhouse.

In fact, humor abounds in the narrative, allowing us to see that though cowboy life at the time was harsh, it had its lighter moments, too. Throughout his account, the narrator maintains a tone detached enough to allow all sides of his tale to be told: the good, the bad, the sad, and the humorous, even if sometimes the incident presents him in an unflattering light.

At times the account becomes almost literary in appearance. Part of that sense is due to the fact that the story works on more than the level of mere narrative. As a literary piece it follows the pattern of the open-ended *bildungsroman*, the novel of experience, for the protagonist begins as a starry-eyed novice and emerges an experienced cowboy by the end. He has matured professionally, but he is also a wiser man at the end because of the hardship and misfortune he has suffered.

On one level the narrative is a direct recounting of the action and accompanying activities, but it also reveals the narrator's developing character as his perceptions grow and mature. We see him judge the people he meets—companions like Sam, the Texas cowboy, or Al, the half-breed Indian suspected of being, and later proved to be, unreliable—and we discern that his notions are astute. Further, even though the piece appears to be a matter-of-fact narrative, the literary polish of the tale is obvious. Adept in the use of language, the author is at ease in writing his story. Interestingly, the narrative echoes some of the elements found in Owen Wister's classic, *The Virginian*. For instance, Sam, the narrator's close companion and mentor, is a Southerner who has also been a Texas cowboy. However, although this author incorporates dialect also, unfortunately it is not one that rings true; it sometimes sounds instead like the bogus Black dialect employed in the literature of that time.

This fresh view of the cattle industry during a crucial period adds important information to our knowledge of the development of the West. The regret is that this material lay ignored for so many years. Appropriately, however, it finds a reading public in time to help celebrate the centennial of the event that it leads up to: statehood for Wyoming, a state well aware of its ranching heritage. Now that the work has come to light, it serves as an important documentation and confirmation of many aspects of cowboy life about which there has been some confusion or even doubt. Further, it does so in a literary yet unassuming manner with a great deal of humor thrown in for good measure. Indeed, one of the most interesting implications of this material is that it shows a verve for life and a diversity of activity that is not always accorded to the life of the open range cowboy. As such, this narrative deserves to take its place among other important acccounts of cowboy life like *We Pointed Them North, A Texas Cowboy*, or *Log of a Cowboy*, for it, too, provides an enlightening description of life during one of the most significant eras of American history: the development of the West.

JAN ROUSH
LAWRENCE CLAYTON

Pullin' Leather

Yes, a cow boy has his troubles and he shore is out of luck,
Out a dozen miles from nowheres and his hoss begins to
    buck.
And he picks a place to practice on some mighty ugly ground,
Fer you'd land amongst the cactus if he ever got you down.

So you aim to keep a straddle and you'll ride him if you can,
'Elst they'll be a dehorned saddle, or they'll be a one armed
    man.
You don't look like much vaquero, he is floppin' yore shirt
    tails,
You have lost yore old somebrero and you've broke some
    finger nails.

People say that pullin' leather don't show ridin' skill. That's
    true.
But you'd like to stick togather till the argyment is through.
When yo're a slippin' and a slidin', you'll admit at all events
If it doesn't show good ridin' that it shows a heap of sense.

When yo're throwed it ain't so pleasant with a dozen miles
    to walk.
No there ain't nobody present, and the hoss of course cain't
    talk.
You are hangin' on and prayin'. You ain't makin' no grand
    stand.
You just aim to keep a stayin' and you'll do the best you can.

Bruce Kiskaddon
*Rhymes of the Ranges
And Other Poems,* © 1947

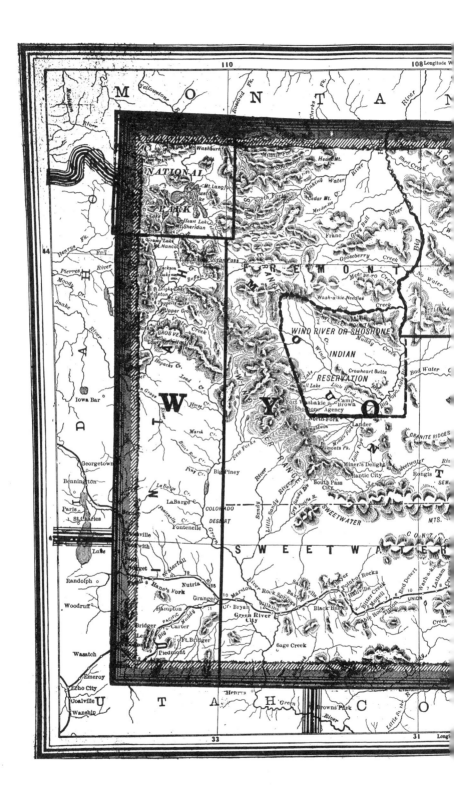

WYOMING
1887

SCALE OF MILES
0 5 10   20   30   40   50   60

Population _ _ _ _ _ _ 20,789
Area, square Miles, _ _ _ _97,575

I Worked on the Sybille Ditch

URING APRIL IN 1884, I took Horace Greeley's advice
and headed for the big, open spaces in Wyoming. After
dodging brakemen night and day, sleeping in boxcars, and
living on crackers part of the time, I arrived in Cheyenne,
after being incarcerated in a boxcar of lumber for twenty-
four hours without food or water. Oh, yes, the old stomach
felt as though it had gone on a prolonged vacation, while
thirst had become a habit. Searching through my pockets, I
found a lone fifty-cent piece, the only cash between me and
starvation. Leaving the station yards, I found an eating joint
where I filled up, but when I left that restaurant, I was broke
and no job in sight.

After consuming that meal, I headed out on the street,
bent on finding a job, and at once my attention was attracted
by hordes of young men tramping the streets. Practically all
wore white felt hats with a broad brim. Some had hat bands
of leather, while others used something resembling a snake
hide. Most all wore high-heeled boots with trousers tucked
in at the tops and spurs with small chains dangling from their
boot heels. Many wore leather trousers minus any seats[1] while
great, large revolvers hung from belts buckled about their
waists, and they traveled in pairs and groups.

This motley crowd of desperate Desmonds[2] was cause
sufficient to make a tenderfoot take to the woods in a hurry,

1

had there been any timber. So desperate these men looked I wouldn't attempt to engage them in conversation, but I would dodge around them that they might have plenty of room on their endless march. After an hour spent in dodging these Desmonds, I spotted a young fellow sitting in the shade of a building, and as he looked civilized, I engaged him in conversation.

"Hello," I said as I approached him. "What kind of people are they?"

"Cowboys," he said, and made room on the box for me. "Are you a cowboy?"

"I never heard of such an animal. What's a cowboy?" I asked.

"Cowboys ride the range after cattle during the summer," he replied. "I'm one. I've been punching cows two summers, but I'll confess those nuts make me tired. Most of them dressed in those outfits are rank tenderfeet and as green as you look."

"How does it happen they're all in town at the same time?"

"The Annual Stock Convention is in session," he replied. "This is the time cow outfits hire men for the summer's work. Want a job punching cows?"

"Not on your life! I'm looking for a job all right, but I haven't any hankering to be mixed up with a bunch of desperate Desmonds like those fellows," I told this cowboy. "I'm wondering where a fellow can find a job. I don't know where I'll sleep tonight or eat when I get hungry," and it was at this juncture a man walked rapidly by.

"There he goes! Catch him. He's hiring men," and I was after that man pronto.

"Are you hiring men?" I asked, as I overhauled him.

He slowed down, and never in my twenty years on earth did I get as nasty a look as this man gave me. At any other time it would have caused a fight or a footrace.

"Yes! I'm hiring men," said the man, and I was subjected

to a critical look. However, this was no time for resentment, as a job was paramount at this time. "What can you do?" he asked.

"I'm a blacksmith by trade, but any old job would fit just now. I'm broke." This simple statement caused the muscles of his expression to relax, and he smiled a sickly smile.

"If you can make good at blacksmithing, I'll give you two dollars a day and feed you. We need a blacksmith out on our irrigation project,[3] eighty miles north." Still he looked at me with an eye of suspicion, as I was rather small and bleached white from my years in a blacksmith shop and coal mines in Iowa. Not yet had I reached my twenty-first birthday, but I would in August.

"I'm only asking for a tryout," I replied. "When do you leave town?"

"The outfit heads north in the morning, leaving from the city corral. Be on hand early," he said and started away.

"Say, Mister, I'm broke and must have a bed and two eats before that time, and I'm wondering what we can do about that?" I asked.

"That's easy! Loan me that watch of yours until we start out on the trail, and I'll advance you a dollar." He handed me a silver dollar, and I handed over that old silver watch I'd had so much trouble keeping away from Union Pacific brakemen. With my dollar in my pocket I returned to my newly found friend, who had watched the entire transaction.

"Kid, you're some fast worker, I'd say," said McClusky. "I reckon you'll make the hill in this country."[4]

"Where can I locate one sleep and two eats for the price of the dollar?" I asked McClusky.

He gave me the desired information, and we parted, not to meet for a period of two years when we found each other on a roundup in northern Wyoming.

That rooming house was found and accommodations secured, though some days later I found I had taken something away from that house I hadn't paid for and didn't want. The balance of the day I spent loafing about the streets watching those tenderfeet hunting jobs; now I knew they weren't dangerous at all and not half so lucky as the recent arrival [namely, Mullins himself].

Punctuality is, and always has been, an institution with me. At the appointed time I was at the corral in company with several other men, and we were all set for that eighty-mile trip north. No, I did not propose to lose out on my first job; besides, I remembered that man had my watch, which must have been worth five dollars.

For four days we plugged along in a cold, drizzling rain which chilled me to the bone. At night we'd stand around a small campfire and try to dry out our clothes and get warm. Then we'd crawl in between wet blankets in our wet tent and shiver all night. This lasted four days and nights; then we reached the main camp of the contractor, a Mr. Bradburg. Here I was handed two pairs of cotton blankets and a suit of underwear, shown a place to sleep, and promptly forgotten until next morning.

The next morning I was taken to the blacksmith shop and told to get busy. I was not long in finding that iron and steel work much the same in Wyoming as it does in Iowa, and quickly I was turning out the work satisfactorily. This first day proved just a tryout, and when it was found I could do their work, I was promptly transferred to a sub-camp run by a man called Nicholas. When duly located in this small camp, I found the outstanding and most important figure in this outfit to be the cook, who was an Englishman. He was fifty years of age and the owner of a beautiful, long whisker that reached his waistband. I soon found that his predominating characteristic was his overgrown temper, and every man, including the boss, must tread lightly while about his cook shack.

I soon established a strong friendship with the cook due to some repairs I made on his cookstove, and after this job he would often call me to his cook shack and invite me to try out some of the choice morsels of food he had concocted in his culinary department. Needless to say, I enjoyed these lunches between times, and while consuming them I would gaze at that nice, long whisker while he would tell me of fearful experiences he'd passed through in the West, causing me to believe he was a dangerous man. As he talked, he would stroke those long whiskers, and I was always on the lookout for one or more hairs in my food. But look as much as I would, I never found one outside of its usual resting place.

During the second day in this camp, I developed an itching that couldn't be satisfied although I used both hands and one foot scratching and digging. When I warmed up in bed, the desire to scratch kept me awake; then one day while the men were out on the ditch and the cook was busy in his shack, off came that shirt, and I took a look inside. There they were, hundreds of them chasing each other up and down the seams of the shirt, all trying to get under cover. In size they resembled a kernel of wheat. Hair-like projections poked out from their sides, which served for locomotion, and how they could get over the country! A dark streak ran down their backs, reminding one of a skunk, while all were fat and greasy.

Slamming the garment on the floor, I let out a whoop that brought friend cook on the run, who after a careful diagnosis labeled them cooties, or the "Native Sons of Wyoming." Whiskers laughed loud and he laughed long, causing me to believe he was hysterical. I will say it was no laughing matter with me, and I patiently waited for the spasm to pass. After cooling down, the cook advised me to get the wash boiler and give them a hot bath, which I promptly did. This enabled me to live in peace for a time; then repeating the hot bath, I was free of cooties.

Most all were young men in this camp, and a most congenial bunch at that. However, there came a day when a great calamity struck the camp like a bolt of lightning out of a clear sky. The trouble came through two miscreants in human form who set their tent just about a mile up Sand Creek from our location, where they dispensed rotgut whiskey and crooked games of cards. The Sunday following the opening of this saloon, several of the boys decided to visit the place and sample their goods, maybe indulge in cards. Jerry, my bunk-mate and friend, was a boy a trifle older than I, and every man in the outfit was his friend. Even our cook liked Jerry as that boy wore a smile that wouldn't come off. It just stuck on his face all the time.

I protested to Jerry and strongly advised him to remain in camp and rest with me; yet over my protest Jerry toddled along with the others and spent the entire day in that hellhole, which proved his undoing altogether. The fellows stopped up at the saloon all day, which caused Mr. Nicholas, our boss, to get nervous, and he asked several of us to go with him to the saloon and help herd those fellows back to camp. On reaching the place we found several of the boys moderately full, others more so, while several were perfectly full and owned the earth. Uniformly, all were broke as those vermin had gypped them out of every white dime they had.

Before returning to camp Jerry had to get a pint of that rotten whiskey for friend cook in payment for past favors. On reaching camp Jerry presented the cook with his bitters. I passed on into our tent and waited for the supper gong. When it did sound, the gang rushed into the mess tent, and all took their places. Entering the place a moment later, I noticed the first thing that all were in a hilarious frame of mind except Jerry, whose face was as black as a thundercloud. Upon inquiring what it was all about, I was informed that the cook and Jerry had had a friendly scuffle, and the cook flopped Jerry. Watching the reaction on Jerry from the distance where I sat, I thought the guying[5] had gone far enough and the fellows should ease up on Jerry; however, I remained quiet. Yet there was no letup, and in a moment Jerry declared in a loud voice that if he couldn't throw the old son of a ——, he could get him the other way.

All knew Jerry wasn't himself, that it was the rotgut

whiskey talking, but knowing the cook as I did, I shyed a glance through the kitchen door and saw the cook grab a rolling pin; then he made a run for Jerry. But the blow he struck at the boy fell short of the mark, and Jerry was unharmed. In a second before he could be restrained, Jerry whipped out an old hog leg[6] and a flame of fire flashed out. The cook crumpled up on the floor, blood oozing from two holes where the pistol ball had passed through his abdomen. I was the first to reach the cook, and we carried him out in the open, but by this time he had become pale and quiet, and it needed no doctor to diagnose the case. The cook passed out the next (Monday) afternoon, and the body was placed in a container ready for transportation to Cheyenne.

Jerry wrenched loose from those who tried to restrain him and ran staggering from camp, heading for the hills. The horse wrangler was out with the horses and mules. Seeing Jerry running bareheaded and staggering, at times falling, and having heard that shot in camp, he surmised that something was wrong. He intercepted Jerry in his flight for his life and caused him to return to camp. Two men guarded Jerry all next day until nine o'clock in the evening, when he was placed on the seat of a spring wagon with his feet securely bound and his wrists corded. Mr. Nicholas rode on one side of Jerry and the bookkeeper on the other. The corpse was placed in the spring wagon, and the drive started for Cheyenne. This was the last we ever saw of Jerry alive.

With a brainstorm raging and my nerves jumpy, I pounded at my anvil next morning but couldn't seem to make any headway with my work. Nothing went right, and I had a notion I would chuck up the job and beat it from an accursed environment where things such as this could happen. With gloomy thoughts chasing themselves through my mind, the sound of a human voice brought me back to earth with a jolt.

"You guys better go down the creek and plant your bad man," said this freighter, who sat on his horse in front of my shop with a quizzical look on his face.

At first his meaning wasn't clear, but after a moment the truth flashed on me that Jerry had been lynched. This was a shock to my youthful nerves as never in the range of my experience had such a thing come under my observation, and it caused a desire to come over me to beat it out of such an accursed environment. The next three hours waiting for the men to come in off the works were the longest ones in my life, yet the time passed and the gang was in camp. Now I related the freighter's story, which caused all to be silent and depressed as Jerry was a well-liked boy and everybody's friend.

The noon meal was eaten in silence and quickly finished; then we drilled down the creek until our eyes contacted a sight never to be forgotten, and I hope I shall never see such another. Before we reached that large cottonwood tree on the bank of Sand Creek, we knew the freighter's story was true, for we could see Jerry's body swaying backward and forward in the breezes coming out of the mountains.[7] Whether right or wrong, the majesty of the law had been vindicated and a crime punished by committing another. The thoughtful man might well ask, why not punish the real miscreants? Yet they were allowed to drive away in peace to other camps, there to continue their damnable work of prostituting our young American manhood.

With all this tragedy rampant in our camp, I lost interest in my work and shortly called for my pay, determined to seek work in fields far removed from the terrible environment where I had spent most of two months. With my savings stowed in an inside pocket, my blanket rolled and tied across my shoulders, and a paper bag filled with food, I struck the trail for Cheyenne, traveling on foot and alone. All through the day I piked along the lonely trail, and as the shades of evening came, I would make camp. Whenever possible I made camp on some creek or near a water hole where I could have water and perhaps a fire.

Otherwise I would make camp out on the hills or on the prairie, where I would munch my food in silence and solitude. Afterwards I would smoke my pipe until I became sleepy, then roll up in my blankets and try to sleep. However, those cold, Wyoming nights with the coyotes making them more hideous by their doleful howls were not conducive to sleep. As the light commenced to come out of the east, I would roll my blankets and start tramping. On this part of the trail there wasn't the first sign of human habitation, and it was a condition to get on a tenderfoot's nerves. After a forty-mile hike I came to Chugwater, and by this time my stock of food had run low and must be replenished at this road ranch. Here I struck the stage line. Now all the way into Cheyenne there was plenty of evidence of human life, and the trip wasn't quite so lonely. The fourth evening I reached Cheyenne, and was I tired and footsore. I bedded down at the old Simmonds Hotel, and the first thing I took a bath and enjoyed a long night's sleep.

While it has been practically fifty years since this experience, every detail stands out clear in my mind, and I have tried very hard to relate correctly all the transactions of my first experience in Wyoming.

---

[1]Apparently Mullins' descriptive term for what is commonly called chaps or leggings.

[2]Probably a reference to William Desmond (1878–1943), an Irish-born American stage and silent-film star. He played in many western and society melodramas and was very popular in the 1920s so would likely have been known to Mullins, who comments in his narrative on the erroneous depiction of cowboy life in movies of the day. See Ephriam Katz, *The Film Encyclopedia* (New York: Putnam, 1979), p. 323.

[3]The Sybille Ditch, part of an early effort to bring water from the Laramie Range through irrigation canals to a poorly watered lowland area. Financed by the Wyoming Development Company to promote settlement by farmers, the system near Wheatland, Wyoming, is still in use.

[4]A metaphorical reference equivalent to "making the grade" or succeeding.

[5]To poke fun. See Eric Partridge, *A Dictionary of Slang and Unconventional English,* 7th ed., 2 vols. in 1 (New York: Macmillan, 1970), p. 364.

[6]Common name for a pistol.

[7]Recounted in a slightly different version by Mrs. Virginia Wolff, wife of a later owner of the Two Bar Ranch at Wheatland, on which the incident occurred. See Harmon Ross Mothershead, *The Swan Land and Cattle Company, Ltd.* (Norman: University of Oklahoma Press, 1971), pp. 167–168.

Blacksmithing at Chugwater

W HEN I REACHED CHEYENNE, my feet were sore, my legs were tired, and my whiskers were long and soiled, yet I was conscious of a feeling of independence as I had fifty dollars stowed away in my clothes. Providing myself with such clothing as I needed, I cleaned up, then started out on a trip I had planned back in Iowa. Often in my youthful days I had listened in on men who had been west, telling their stories of Cheyenne and its famous Gold Room. [1]

I promised myself that I would see this famous Gold Room, now a matter of history. My first voyage was to search out this place, which was easily found. Entering this room which had been enshrined in my mind as being almost sacred, my youthful dreams were smashed. Instead of finding a gilded palace with its tinkling glasses and happy laughing men and women, I found the Gold Room to be just an overgrown saloon like all the rest of them. It, too, had its long bar and mirrors, its foot rail and cuspidors, while men were lined up in front of the bar drinking just plain beer.

Many gambling games were scattered about the place, but only a few were in operation. On a table I saw a pile of gold and silver coins as large as a half bushel basket. Most of the men were playing at this game, trying to extract coin from that pile by betting. However, most of them seemed to lose, and it occurred to me that it took a smart man to win at that game, so that let me out. While looking about, I saw men stake and lose hundreds of dollars, while a few would win heavily on a turn of the card. I meditated as I watched the game and vowed a vow that under no circumstances would my money be bet on games of chance; even now, forty-eight years later, I have never broken that vow.

Since landing in Wyoming, I had heard considerable talk about cow ranches and cowboys, and it had proved interesting, so much so that I resolved to try out the business if I could land a job. Going deeper into the subject, I learned there were wagons to keep in repair and work horses to be shod, while branding irons must be repaired and new ones made, which called for mechanical skill such as I had for sale. With this thought in mind, I started out looking for work in some cow outfit. Having decided to try out the cattle outfits, I made some inquiry and was directed to the main office of the Swan Land and Cattle Company.[2] I was told this was the largest outfit in Wyoming, and it was thought I would stand the best show with them.

In 1884 Cheyenne wasn't what it is now in 1932, and I experienced no trouble finding their office. Entering the place, I found one lone man, sitting at a desk looking over papers. It was with considerable hesitation that I approached this man and asked if his company could use a blacksmith.

As he turned in his chair to note the interruption, I knew I was in the presence of a Scotchman, as I had spent three years in a Scotch family and amongst many Scotchmen. During this time I had acquired considerable of the Scotch brogue, which doubtless helped a lot in securing me a job at this time.

Observing a bald-faced kid standing before him asking for a man–size job caused him to smile, and he asked if I were a blacksmith. Taking on a slight Scotch accent, I told of my experience with the Scotch blacksmith, which caused his eyes to twinkle. He presently assured me that he did have a job for me at fifty a month and keep. However, it would be necessary to go out to Chugwater to the main ranch. Early next morning Mr. Al Bowie, Swan's general manager, drove a pair of prancing roadsters hitched to a buckboard up to the hotel, and I climbed aboard and hit the trail for Chugwater. By noon we reached the ranch and had dinner, after which Mr. Bowie gave his ranch foreman some instructions relative to my activities; then he returned to Cheyenne.

My new boss took me to the shop and, after giving me some instructions about my work and the collection of money, left me to work out my own salvation. Well, that forge and new tools with plenty of good blacksmith coal looked inviting, and shortly the sparks were flying while the anvil was giving off its silvery peals, the sweetest music of all music and in perfect harmony with my thoughts.

Within an hour a stage driver known as George Lathrop led a pair of stage horses into the shop and requested they be re-shod on the front feet. However, on seeing just a runt of a kid officiating, he had some hestiation about having the shoeing done. It seemed shoeing stage horses was particular work and was usually done by older and more experienced blacksmiths. He did decide, however, to allow me to proceed with the shoeing, but he kept a strict watch on my activities all through the job.

First I removed the old shoes and carefully pared off all surplus hoof; then I sharpened the calks and fitted the shoes to the hoofs. It was amusing to watch Mr. Lathrop, who looked as though he thought I might possibly cut off a hoof. As I started driving nails through the shoe and hoof, Mr. Lathrop was on the watch; then after a little while he smiled, so the work must have met with his approval. This stage driver gave me much helpful advice regarding the shoeing of road horses, and through this very help I became a better horseshoer. My experience during the summer with Mr. Lathrop taught me there was no better stage driver than he; however, Tom Duffy, his driving partner, gave him a close run for honors.

George Lathrop was a pioneer in Wyoming and had a

hand in shaping the affairs of the Territory. Only two years
ago the citizens of Lusk raised a monument to his memory
south of Lusk on the old Black Hills Trail, under which his
ashes repose.

The owner of this stage line, Mr. Russell Thorp, often
came into the shop on his trips over the line while awaiting
the change of horses. One stage every day each way was the
schedule, and while waiting for the change of horses the
passengers would get out and walk about, often coming into
the shop. Through this, I met many old-timers and pioneers.[3]
Hiram B. Kelly, the original owner of the Chugwater Ranch,
would visit in the shop by the hour, and, puncher-like, he'd
always be whittling a stick. E. W. Whitcomb often visited
in the shop. Colin Hunter, of northern Wyoming, would
often stretch his legs about the shop. Charley F. Coffee, the
owner of an outfit in Hat Creek Basin but at the present time
a banker in Chadron, Nebraska, was a visitor in the shop.
U.S. Senator John B. Kendrick,[4] of the OW and 76 outfits,
worked on roundups with me. Hard Luck, Lee Moore, T.
B. Hord, Billy Irwin [Irvine?], Frank Lusk,[5] Sam Groves of
the Fiddleback,[6] Billy Keating[7] of the 4W,[8] Curtis Spaugh of
the OS, Henry Blair of the Hoe,[9] U.S. Senator and former
Governor Joseph M. Carey, J. T. Williams of Douglas, former Governor DeForest Richards, former Senator Francis E.
Warren, and many other prominent citizens were well known
to me. This list could be indefinitely extended, but what's
the use as most of these men are doing last relief.[10]

I had been in this shop less than a week when work commenced to pile up and not a moment to spare. Visitors were
plentiful, yet I had only time to extend a friendly "Howdy"
and go on with my work. However, a man did show up in
the shop who caused me to arrest my work and give him
some attention. In build this man was about my size, only a
dozen years older. He had a red face so closely shaven it
looked as if the skin would crack and bleed. He had the nicest
white teeth, furthermore, and they weren't false ones.

The Cheyenne–Deadwood Stage taken near Chugwater in 1884, the same year that Mullins did repairs on the stage as a blacksmith at the Swan Company there. *Photo courtesy of Priscilla Hogan.*

When I handed him my friendly "Howdy," he paid no attention to me but just glared around the shop, which made me nervous. Believing him to be some cowboy just rubbering, I gave him no further attention but continued with my work. Presently he turned his attention to me, and the way he could say things, in the broadest Scotch, indicated to me that his tongue was loose at both ends for the words rolled out in a continuous stream. He gave me more orders in two minutes than I could remember in two weeks, and in so doing, his eyes snapped faster than a toad's in fly time. So interesting was his line of talk, I laid my hammer on the anvil, placed my foot on the anvil block, and waited until he ran dry, returning his glare with interest.

"Who are you, that you come in here interfering with my work?" I asked this wild man. "If my work don't suit you, and you have a notion that you can do it better, hop to it as I'm about through. I don't like such guff, and I don't propose to let anyone get by with it," I pointedly told him, and as my speech progressed, my temperature rose and, by the time I was through, I was ready for a fight. As I spoke, I used some of his own Scotch brogue; then I noticed the muscles of expression relax. The corners of his mouth receded toward his ears while his eyes began to sparkle, and the fool Scotchman was laughing at me.

"Do ye nae ken, I'm Duncan Grant,[11] Mr. Bowie's assistant manager, and hoo de ye like the job?"

"When one learns who all the bosses and managers are that interfere with the work, it may not be so bad," I shot at him.

"I ken ye're all reight, lad; de they kape ye busy?" he asked.

"Do I look like I had been loafing? I could use a helper if the bloomin' outfit wasn't so tight."

"What de ye want done? I'm nae te gude te help a wee mite," declared this assistant manager.

"Shed your coat, and I'll show you what I want done,"

I told him in a none too friendly tone of voice. He did shed his coat and swung onto the handle of the sledge hammer, and in a few minutes the sweat was pouring down his red face. This assistant manager hung around the shop for two days helping all he could, and he seemed to enjoy his work. In a short time we became regular buddies, and in the future if I had any troubles, Duncan Grant was the one to iron them out in a satisfactory way. After the second day, Duncan Grant faded away, I suppose to attend to his regular duties. All through the summer, however, it was impossible for him to remain away from the shop for any extended time. He seemed to love this mechanical work; besides, he could get his fill of it without losing caste with his men. As I thought it over, I didn't wonder that this man had risen from a regular puncher to the top job he held. Often I'd quiz Duncan about his cowboys, a sight I'd never yet seen.

"Ye nade na mind the cowboys. Ye'll hae ye'r day before fall," he declared; and sure enough, I did "hae me day."

---

[1]A bar, gambling house and variety theatre established in 1867. Its reputation was glamorous, but it was also noted for gunfights and gilded ladies and known as a center of turbulence. See "Decrepit Building Now Being Wrecked Was Far Famed Gold Room of Early Day Cheyenne," *Cheyenne State Leader,* Nov. 24, 1936.

[2]Founded by Alexander Swan in 1883. The company had vast holdings that extended from Fort Steele, Wyoming, to Ogallala, Nebraska. Their holdings in Laramie County, headquartered at Chugwater, were extensive: the ranch controlled over 600,000 acres of land and had 120,000 head of cattle. See Ernest Staples Osgood, *The Day of the Cattlemen,* 1929, rpt. (Chicago: Univ. of Chicago Press, 1957), pp. 97–99, 192, 222, and a map following p. 204. See also *Wyoming: A Guide to Its History, Highways, and People,* 1949, rpt. with introduction by T. A. Larson (Lincoln: University of Nebraska Press, 1981), pp. 290–291.

[3]A virtual who's who of the early range. Mullins apparently met and worked with many such people who later were instrumental in developing the territory. A careful check of the records indicates that Mullins' recollections are accurate.

[4]Later a governor of Wyoming and U.S. Senator. Kendrick was a former trail driver acquainted with many of the cowboys of the day. He was president of the Wyoming Stock Growers Association in 1914 when he asked Harry E. Crain to put together a collection of letters documenting

the history of range life in early Wyoming. See Louis Pelzer, *Cattleman's Frontier* (Glendale, California: The Arthur H. Clark Company, 1936), pp. 48–49; "The Texas Trail," *Cheyenne State Leader,* December 10, 1916; and *Wyoming: A Guide,* pp. 100, 213, 324.

⁵The man after whom the town of Lusk, Wyoming, was named. See *Wyoming: A Guide,* p. 224. See also other materials on Lusk on page 34 of the text.

⁶One of the earliest ranches in this area. It was established in 1879 on the Cheyenne River approximately eight miles from the 4W Ranch. Col. E. F. Tillotson, formerly stationed at Fort Fetterman, was the original owner. See *Pioneering on the Cheyenne River,* comp. Robber's Roost Historical Society (Lusk, Wyoming: *Lusk Herald,* 1947), pp. 13–14.

⁷A native Texan and the foreman of the 4W Ranch. He later bought the ULA Ranch. See *Pioneering on the Cheyenne River,* p. 6.

⁸Established by the Hammond Cattle Company around 1880. Located on the Cheyenne River approximately twelve miles from the AU7 Ranch, the 4W Ranch ranged about 10,000 head of cattle. Billy Keating was its foreman. See *Pioneering on the Cheyenne River,* pp. 8–9.

⁹Established in 1880 on Powder River near the mouth of Nine Mile Creek. George Wellman, an early foreman, was one of the victims of the Johnson County War in 1892. See Maurice Frink, *Cow Country Cavalcade: Eighty Years of the Wyoming Stock Growers Association* (Denver: Old West Publishing, 1954), p. 71.

¹⁰An expression synonymous with taking one's last journey, i.e., death.

¹¹One of several managers of the Swan Land and Cattle Company. See *The Swan Land and Cattle Company, Ltd.,* p. 167.

A Cowboy for a Day

EARLY IN OCTOBER Duncan Grant came in the shop with a smile spread over his face and informed me the pasture would be rounded up in a few days and he would desire my help for the day with the roundup. Happy! The word would not express my condition of mind. Now I was to enjoy my fondest dream. For one day I was to mount the hurricane deck[1] of a bronco or cayuse[2] and chase the festive bovines over the badlands and prairie to be a real cowboy for one, glorious day.

Shortly thereafter, late one afternoon the outfit pulled into the corral by the shop and made camp. Hurriedly I completed my work, locked the shop for the night, and joined the cowboys in camp. Furthermore, I remained in camp just as long as anyone would talk to me. At last finding myself deserted, I returned to the ranch and climbed into my own bunk, but try as much as I could, sleep would not come.

Each time I closed my eyes, great herds were passing before me, driven by yelping cowboys. I could see cowboys riding bucking broncos, roping cattle and calves, and branding calves, all of which made a beautiful picture in my imagination. After a time, however, the cowboys and cattle grew dim, and presently I slumbered.

When the cook called "chuck" at three next morning, I was in line with my tin cup and plate, ready for my portion of cowboy grub. With my cup filled with black coffee strong enough to walk and my plate piled with fried beefsteak and gravy, I dropped on the ground, cowboy style, and ate my breakfast.

With this operation finished, all the punchers unloosed their ropes from the saddles and made ready to lasso their horses. As I stood watching, it seemed marvelous how a puncher could throw his rope and catch one particular horse without catching a dozen others as they were jammed tight together and the older horses would sometimes duck or dodge the rope. However, it looked easy, especially for Duncan as he roped out a long-legged bay horse and instructed me to saddle him.

That horse looked good to me; however, had I known some of his fine qualities there would have been no cow-punching for me that day. With the large experience I had had shoeing horses, fear of them had been eliminated, and when the time came to mount, I promptly attempted to do so—from the wrong side. The horse shied away from me, which caused the punchers to enjoy their first laugh at my expense. Duncan told me to mount from the left side of the horse as only Indians mounted from the right side.

After this mistake, I quickly mounted from the left side, and immediately things began to happen so fast I lost track of events altogether. For a time, mind, muscle, and action were concentrated in trying to stay on top of that horse. The first thing the bronc did was to jump toward the sky and then hit the ground with such a jolt it almost loosened my hold on the saddle horn; I thought my neck was unjointed and every bone in my body jammed. The bronc had his head stowed away between his front legs, his back curved like a barrel, and his legs as stiff as a fence post. Each time he hit the ground, he gave an unearthly cough or bellow, which caused me to think he had a bad cold and shouldn't have been ridden as it might cause him to develop pneumonia. At the first ascension, I had lost my hat and both stirrups; I let go of the bridle reins, which dangled beside his head, and I with both hands grabbed the saddlehorn with a death grip. One thought alone percolated my consciousness and that was that if that bronc dumped me, he would get away with the saddle and my big day would be spoiled. I froze tightly to the saddle horn, determined that if I went off, it would go with me, and then it could be placed on another horse. Up and down, round and round, went the bronc and I, my muscles exerted to the limit, holding on. After several ascensions, the bronc decided it was no use, so he eased up on his pestications, and for the remainder of the day he was a good horse.

But what of the spectators? All were yelling their heads off, offering some of the rottenest advice ever handed out to a tenderfoot: "Jump off," "Pull leather, Cowboy," "Whip him over the head," "Ride him, Cowboy," and other equally instructive suggestions. Their suggestions, however, passed unnoticed as I was entirely too busy to listen to them. When the horse quit bucking and quiet was restored, the punchers gathered around and offered their congratulations as a rank tenderfoot had done a thing many of them could not do, namely, stick on that outlaw bronc. Yet there was considerable disappointment, as every mother's son of them had expected the kid blacksmith to hit the ground. Duncan edged into where I was sitting with a grin on that red face of his, and I then realized that I had been framed. However, I was so elated to think I had stayed with both horse and saddle that this knowledge failed to dampen my ardor in the least.

With this excitement over, the business of the day was begun. Duncan divided the men into four bunches, and they started out in four directions on a keen run, Duncan leading one bunch. Chasing along with his bunch of cowboys, it seemed to me Duncan had gone plumb crazy the way he ran his horse up and down hill, over badlands, sagebrush flats, ditches, and washouts in all manner of country, including prairie dog towns.

My bronc knew what was expected of him even if I didn't,

and despite my pulling and tugging at the bridle rein, he kept up with the procession, with me still clinging to the saddle-horn. We finally came to a wire fence and stopped while the horses rested and got their second wind, and the punchers took time to recinch their saddles as the race had gaunted the horses. After a rest and a smoke, all mounted, and it appeared we were ready for the second spasm. Duncan had the men ride along the fence both ways until they contacted the other men; then they drove all the cattle found toward camp, or our starting place. By ten o'clock the cattle were on the roundup ground, about three thousand head in the herd. Duncan instructed a few men to hold the cattle while the rest raced to camp for a change of horses.

Duncan this time roped a small black pony and told me to saddle him; then he caught one, an exact match for the black I had, and saddled him for himself. I saddled the horse but had some hesitation about mounting him as I remembered my morning's experience.

"Climb on him, Cowboy," shouted Duncan. "He couldn't buck off a saddle blanket."

I did climb on, and the pony trotted away as quietly as Mary's little lamb. When we reached the roundup ground, Duncan invited me to help him cut out cows and calves, whatever that was. I followed him into the herd, and we were soon shooting[3] an old cow with her calf toward the outside.

In a minute or so we had them a few yards from the herd when the blooming calf undertook to go back into it, and believe it or not, on the watch when the calf whirled around, my pony gave a side jump that came near unseating me and landed right in the calf's path, nosing it back. The calf turned toward the prairie and a fifty-foot run ensued, the pony getting in ahead of the calf and turning it back to its mother. This running, stopping, and dodging continued until the calf was once more beside its mother, and in the meantime the punchers were yelling themselves hoarse. I found this little black streak of lightning harder to stick on than the bucking bronc had been, yet with the aid of the saddlehorn I did stick to the saddle.

Once more the cowboys were howling themselves hoarse, Duncan with the rest. I rearranged myself in the saddle, smiled at them, and waited for further instructions, which came from Duncan in the form of suggestions and a demonstration as to the proper way to cut out or carve cattle. As I helped hold the herd, the punchers would edge up to me and admire my mount as he was supposed to be one of the top cow horses of the territory and beyond monetary value. I was told none of the men ever rode either of those little black streaks as they were the special property of Mr. Grant and reserved for his use.

I was positively sure the little black horse had forgotten more about cattle than I would ever know, and just why Duncan invited me to ride him was beyond understanding; however, I had my own private ideas about Mr. Grant and the matter of the horse. I had shown him a good time at a kind of work that he thoroughly enjoyed, even though it cost him a lot of sweat. In turn he was showing me for one day a perfectly hot time at a job I was crazy about. This experience caused a desire to punch cows to percolate through my system, and it was going to take about five years to get it out.

With the cows and calves cleaned out of the herd, the fat cattle were cut out and bunched, then later thrown in the beef herd which the outfit was holding. The cows and calves were driven into the branding pen and the calves branded, after which they were turned back in the pasture to loaf for another year. With the work completed, we broke camp and the outfit headed down the road submerged in a cloud of dust; this was the end of cowboy life for me at this time.

Yet not the end, either, for the next two or three days found me developing a cranky disposition hard to overcome. Every muscle and tendon in my body was sore, while my bones felt all jammed and wouldn't function. I could neither lie down, sit, nor stand with comfort, and it was a job to keep on living. Despite my soreness I kept on working, and as I thought of that long-legged bronc and that little black streak of lightning, I was forced to grin triumphantly to myself, in spite of my suffering.

A short time thereafter Duncan entered the shop, his face as long as a fiddle, and seeing his serious look, I asked, "Are you grieving because you have treated me so rotten?"

"Nae, lad, nane o' that. But I hae me orders to close the shop for the winter," he said mournfully. "If ye de nae mind, ye can gae back hame on a cattle train and nae fare to pay. The ranch boss will find a horse for ye to gang into Cheyenne. Ye can come back i' the spring, and ye'll receive a raise of ten a month."

I did not agree to come back, but I did tell him that if I worked at my trade it would be for him. A day or two later I found myself stowed away in a caboose hitched to thirty cars loaded with fine beef steers, rambling along toward Chicago.

This was my last meeting with Duncan Grant, who was ever my idea of a real man. I enjoyed knowing and for a time associating with Duncan Grant, although at our first meeting things had not been so pleasant. In reviewing my association with many men in my walks of life, I have failed utterly to find many whom I regard with more respect than Duncan Grant, and my acquaintance with him has been one of the milestones that have made life worth living.

---

[1]A slang expression used to indicate the back of a horse. See, for example, Charles Siringo, *A Texas Cowboy, or Fifteen Years on the Hurricane Deck of a Spanish Pony*, 1885, rpt. (Lincoln: University of Nebraska Press, 1979).
[2]Two slang expressions for *horse*.
[3]A slang expression for separating one kind of cattle (steers, calves, bulls, etc.) from the rest of the herd. The term was replaced by *cutting* or *separating*.

With the AU7 Outfit

ON THE WAY TO CHICAGO over the good old Union Pacific, I had a lot of time to think things over. I wouldn't have exchanged my summer's experience for anything in this big world, and my heart was set on being a real cowboy the next year.

On this trip with me were three cowboys who accompanied the shipment for the purpose of prodding up some steers who had decided to lie down and take a nap in transit. The cowboys were to see that the cattle were properly fed, watered, and rested at given points along the route. They were to turn the shipment over to the commission men in Chicago and then return to the home ranch in Wyoming.

We ran into the stockyards at Chicago one morning early just after a warm rain, which caused the yards to be anything but a desirable place. After delivering our shipment, we had a meal in a nearby restaurant, then started our trip up town, and what a trip!

We mounted a small streetcar drawn by horses and driven by a man who stood on the front end of the car. This man started into a long canyon that seemed to have no end. While on our way up town, we saw thousands, then other thousands of people rushing about in different directions at a speed one might ordinarily take were he going to a fire or hunting a doctor. After a long time we came to our destination, which proved to be the Burlington depot. Now the canyons were much deeper and the people more numerous, and I stuck close to the cowboys lest I get lost in that milling mass of humanity and never see Wyoming again.

Once in the train I found it much easier to breathe as the fear of getting lost had vanished. We were headed west, and after several hours of reckless riding, our train pulled up in Ottumea, Iowa. As I left the train at this place, my attention was attracted to hordes of men wearing white plug hats. On inquiry, I learned they were Cleveland Democrats. It seemed some fellow in New York by the name of Grover Cleveland wanted to be President of the United States, and the white plug hats were his distinctive badge. I remembered I had passed my twenty-first birthday and was a legal voter. I then remembered that my father was a Kentucky Democrat, so I bought a white plug hat, and at the proper time I cast my first vote for Grover Cleveland.

The winter was spent working in the mines at What Cheer, and I had a rollicking good time amongst former associates; yet, when the grass commenced to turn green and the little robins were hopping about amidst the shrubbery, my feet got itchy, and presently I was in the cars beating it for Cheyenne and the big open spaces which had now become a part of my life. On this trip to the West, there was no riding in boxcars loaded with lumber, but I rode on the plush-bottomed seats which were none too good for me as I had plenty of kale.[1] Before I left Omaha, I also had a small box filled with choice morsels of food.

While gliding over the prairies west of Omaha on the old Union Pacific, my attention was attracted to a long, lanky fellow lounging in his seat opposite me, and my guess was that he was a cowboy. I scraped an acquaintance with this man and learned from his speech that he was a Southerner, and a much older man than I. He proved to be a Texas cowpuncher named Sam Mathers now on his way to Cheyenne, and he informed me that he was aiming to punch cows during the summer for the AU7 outfit[2] on the Cheyenne River, a place where he'd worked during the past year.

I willingly related my own experiences of the past year, speaking of the long-legged bronc and the little black streak of lightning and what they had tried to do to me, and Sam Mathers just broke down and haw-hawed; and he, like the other cowpunchers, told me to hang onto my nerve.

So friendly we became that I asked Sam to help me eat up that batch of grub. While having our smoke after the feed, we had a long talk about cowboys and cowboy life, a work Sam had followed all his life. Before reaching Cheyenne, Sam had adopted me as his special charge, and he took upon himself the responsibility of finding me a job in a real outfit.

Landing in Cheyenne we dismounted from the train and presently found ourselves bedded down in the old Simmonds House, a popular bed ground for punchers. It was evident we were early for the annual stock convention, so we had a lot of idle time on our hands, which was largely spent in watching the trains come in and in observing cowboys and would-be cowboys disgorge from these trains. While most of these fellows were rank tenderfeet, they were nevertheless dressed in cowboy outfits. These would-be cowboys looked green, they smelled green, and they were green. After a batch of them would arrive, Sam would beef about them until the next batch came in. He would declare those tenderfeet had never seen a cow outside of some barnyard or a farm pasture. Yet to watch them as they stepped from the trains, they would make people believe they were old-time cowpunchers.

Hotels, boarding and rooming houses, gambling joints, saloons, and all kindred places were rapidly filled, and by the time the Stock Growers Convention[3] started, men were tramping the streets with nowhere to lay their heads. We noticed, however, that drunkenness was conspicuous by its absence. During our entire time in Cheyenne we never saw one drunk; however, there was plenty of gambling going on day and night.[4]

During the first day of the convention, Sam dropped out of sight, and it seemed as if he'd strayed, been lost, or stolen, as he didn't show up at the hotel for several hours. Eventually he did come into the office and immediately made a rush for me.

"He sho' am heah, honey," Sam declared excitedly. "Ah's done got my ole job back." Then he took me by the arm and all but dragged me from the place and headed for the Gold Room.

"That am him," declared Sam, pointing to a tall, bow-legged man with a heavy mustache and keen blue eyes that were capable of looking right through a cowpuncher. If in a good humor, this man had a lovely disposition and a smile that warmed one's heart, but if angry, it was an entirely different story. However, I fell sufficiently within his good graces to be taken on as a ranch employee and this is how it happened.

Sam and I entered the Gold Room, and in a moment Mr. Crawford spied us and came to where we were. Sam in his awkward cowpuncher way introduced us, and we shook hands. Being busy with some game, Mr. Crawford instructed us to meet him in an hour at some place he named and returned to his game and friends. I noticed, however, that he gave me a peculiar look as he left us, and to me it didn't look so good. Sam noticed this, too, and it actually made him sick as it seemed to preclude a successful conclusion to his desired scheme of having me with him on the AU7 outfit. While it would be to my advantage to work with Sam, the prospect of failing did not matter to me so much as I knew a job was awaiting me at Chugwater at better wages than cowpunchers received. However, it wasn't a matter of wages so much that counted as it was my desire to work as a cowpuncher in a regular outfit.

James B. Crawford was foreman of the AU7 outfit, which was located two hundred and twenty-five miles north of Cheyenne on the Cheyenne River at the mouth of Lodge Pole

Creek. He was known as a capable cowman and was often called into consultation by officials of the Stock Growers Association, his advice always being accepted as expert and sound. It seemed that his was one of the keenest minds in the country on matters connected with the cattle business. For the next three years I was to be closely connected with this man, and had it not been for his decided favoritism to Texas men, he would have measured up to all my ideas of what a man should be.

Sam and I were at the appointed place on time, and in a moment Mr. Crawford joined us. He asked me many questions about my previous experiences at blacksmithing and what experience, if any, I had had at cowpunching. I spoke of my various experiences at blacksmithing, then rather boastingly I told of my one big day of working on a roundup. While I was telling of the long-legged bronc and the little black streak and what they did to me, his reserve broke down, and he laughed heartily. In less than twenty minutes I was hired at forty a month[5] and doomed to walk all that distance to the ranch.

Jim, as he was familiarly known to everyone, became most friendly and offered to loan us money, as he must have had a notion we were broke. In fact he instructed us to have a good time while we had a chance. He told me of a nice little shop he'd had built at the ranch but for which he had not as yet purchased the equipment. It was my business to figure out a complete list of what would be needed, and the next day he and I were to do the shopping for this outfit.

This offer of money was mighty nice of Mr. Crawford, but fortunately for us we had sufficient for our needs over the period of waiting. He and I met at a hardware store next morning as agreed and, without waste of words or time, went over the list I had prepared. Scrutinizing my list carefully, then asking many questions, Jim found everything in order except a bag of blacksmith coal which he crossed out, claiming that the Cheyenne River country was full of coal.

When we had completed this feature of the shopping, Jim asked me if I had a cowpuncher outfit.

"No," I replied. "I don't even know what makes up an outfit, much less own one."

"Most tenderfeet learn that first," Jim replied, with a smile at my honest ignorance. He selected an outfit for me which was going to set me back one hundred and fifty bucks, making it evident to me that I would be in debt for some time to come. I noticed that while selecting my bed he failed to get a pillow, yet he ordered a grain sack. When I called Sam's attention to this oversight later, he just had another laugh at my expense; then he explained that the bag was to carry my clothes, tobacco, and whatever I needed, and that this war bag was also to be used as a pillow.

Mr. Crawford seemed so friendly at this time I had a notion he'd been talking with Duncan Grant, whom I had failed to meet up until this time. He now spoke of the probable date of sailing for the ranch, then, instructing us to keep in touch with him, left us to entertain ourselves in our own way.

Sam and I milled around town, watching tenderfeet hunt jobs, and with many of them it was a heartbreaking job. Many of them had come from distant states and paid their railroad fare; then after buying those cowboy outfits they found themselves broke with no job nor any in sight. Sam scolded by the hour about these imitation cowboys, yet in his big, generous heart he was sorry for them. Often we staked some boy to a meal; then Sam would throw in a lot of advice. He would instruct him to sell his outfit back to the store and seek work elsewhere. It was heartbreaking to watch these boys beg work from every cowman they met, but we thought this very experience might prove more useful to them than a job punching cows at thirty a month.

The last afternoon in town was at hand, and here came Mr. Crawford hunting us. He declared that he had hired twenty men and that we were to strike the trail the next morning. These new men Sam and I had not contacted as yet but would the next morning.

On that April morning now forty-seven years past, we were at the corral which I had left one year before on my trip to Chugwater. The whole gang was at hand, and after hitching the teams to those two overloaded wagons, we headed out on the trail for the home ranch. Before we'd reach there, we would be tired, footsore, and dirty.

" 'Pears like they're a right smart bunch," declared Sam as we trailed along, walking mostly in pairs. The fact of the matter was, it was a fine cross-section of young American manhood. This was especially true, from a physical standpoint, of one young man who claimed to be a half-breed Indian, and who looked the part. All the way to the ranch Al would have us feeling his biceps, and he would tell us how handy he was with boxing gloves and how he had stood up with Harry Hynds[6] of Cheyenne, who couldn't stop him.

While in Cheyenne the year before, I had been in Harry's blacksmith shop, and I personally knew that the man Harry couldn't stop must be some go-getter. Back in Iowa I had had a lot of experience with boxing gloves. In fact, many times my face had been so sore from being smashed up with gloves that I couldn't shave it for a week. Boxing was a sport I dearly loved and still do, but I learned early in my experience that I could neither see nor move quickly enough to become a good pug, which barred me from the profession. I seldom, if ever, spoke of this boxing, and now that we had a regular pug in the outfit, I found it good policy to keep quiet altogether and let Al put his Sandy across.

Our noon camp the first day was made on the banks of some small creek, where the horses were fed and rested while we tenderfeet filled up and presently resumed our journey. The night camp was a very nice place, and by this time we were a trifle weary from the day's tramp. But after the evening meal our tongues loosened, and it seemed everyone wanted to talk.

Presently Sam nudged me and said, "You all bettar learn how to fix yo baid." This statement by Sam caused most of the boys to sit up and take notice, as most of them were as green about such things as I was. We watched carefully Sam's method of preparing his bed, which proved to be quite a feat. When completed, the bed resembled a large bag, and one must get into it feet first at the head end, over which a long flap of tarpaulin extended.

In a bed properly made down, one can sleep dry all through a long, rainy night without tent or other protection. It is the puncher's first duty upon rising to roll his bed into a compact roll, then tie it tight with ropes and toss it over by the bed wagon.

The second evening on the trail we camped at Chugwater near my old shop, which I found locked, with cobwebs covering the windows. It was evident no one had worked in the shop since my departure the last October. While here I was reminded of a circumstance which had happened the last year which had knocked all the ambition out of me, if I ever had had any, to be a soldier. It was during one of the hottest days of the summer that a six-mule team and driver, a commissioned officer, and twenty new recruits drove into the corral and made camp.

Bringing up the rear of this caravan were two unarmed soldiers, each carrying a hunk of cordwood, while two soldiers with fixed bayonets drilled along behind them, presumably to prod them along. Reaching the campground, the prisoners dropped their sticks of wood and unhitched and fed the mules. Next they built a fire, after which they brought water for the cook. With this chore completed, they picked up their chunks of wood and walked a beat until the cook called "Chuck."

After the meal those boys picked up their sticks of wood and walked a beat while the others lay around in the shade and slept an hour. At the appointed time, these men did all the work in breaking camp, and the last I saw of them they were drilling down the road carrying their hunks of wood and submerged in a cloud of dust. So much for leaving guard duty the night before and going to a road ranch and getting drunk. It was the army's way of discipline, and now they were paying.

The next camp of any importance was made at old Fort Laramie. We fully expected to find hundreds of soldiers at this place; however, it was almost deserted as no one was to be seen but a few caretakers. It seemed the Indians had been rounded up and placed on the reservation.

Near the fort we noticed four posts a matter of nine feet high with a small platform on top. We were told this was the grave of Fallen Leaf, the daughter of some former warrior chief, who loved an army officer too well, if not wisely.

In another day or two we found ourselves drilling up Rawhide Creek, said to have received its name from an event taking place on its bank during the California gold rush in 1849. As the story goes, a party of people in some eastern site banded themselves together to go to California in search of gold or other misfortune. Amongst their number was a boastful young man who was fired with an ambition to kill an Indian, declaring he would do so at the first opportunity after leaving the confines of civilization. It was on this creek he found his Indian, and true to his boast he shot a hole through a friendly Indian. Soon the tribe of whom this Indian was a member learned the truth of the shooting, and here they came many strong, demanding that the guilty man be given up to them. This the white man refused to do until it became evident the entire caravan would be massacred. The guilty man was pointed out and a deed was consummated which has gone down in history as being the most cruel of all torture. It was said he was flayed while alive. How true the story is no one knows absolutely. Yet one of the oldest men in that country recited this story to me in 1885 as being true.

---

[1] A slang expression for money. See Lester V. Berrey and Melvin Vandenbark, *The American Thesaurus of Slang* (New York: Thomas Y. Crowell, 1953), p. 523.

[2] A ranch established about 1880 on the mouth of Snyder Creek. The Suffolk Cattle Company owned the ranch, ranging cattle on the Cheyenne River and its tributaries. J. B. Thomas was the original manager. The ranch is still in existence today. See *Pioneering on the Cheyenne River,* pp. 10–11; and Elsie Carlson Stokes, "A History of the AU7" *Bits and Pieces* (January/February, 1971), pp. 21–28.

[3] Originally organized as the Laramie County Stock Growers Association on November 29, 1873. The group later became known as the Wyoming Stock Growers Association in 1879. The group was a powerful organization that oversaw the roundups on the open ranges and supported political causes affecting cattlemen. The records of the Stock Growers Association are housed at the University of Wyoming in Laramie. See Osgood, pp. 12–121. See also Cheyenne *Daily Leader,* May 2, 1874 (Osgood 120, Note 11); and *Wyoming: A Guide,* pp. 99, 100, 189, 190.

[4] A passion with many frontiersmen. The cowboy was as much apt to gamble as were miners and others. See Paul I. Wellman, *The Trampling Herd* (New York: Doubleday, 1951), pp. 255–258.

[5] A good wage. Thirty dollars a month was fairly common pay in that day for cowboys.

[6] Famous boxer from Cheyenne as well as one of the "most skilled blacksmiths" in early Wyoming. He built and for many years owned the Plains Hotel in Cheyenne. See *Wyoming: A Guide,* pp. 156–157. The term "pug" used by Mullins is a shortened version of *pugilist.*

A Cowboy Welcome

DAY AFTER DAY WE trudged over this long trail, and now our feet commenced to get sore and our legs tired, yet in a way we were repaid for all this grief by passing over a country that was perfectly lovely at this time of year. The green grass spread out in all directions as far as vision would carry, reminding one of a vast, green velvet carpet, while many cattle, a few horses, and numbers of antelope could be seen grazing. Many young calves were to be seen frisking around their mothers, enjoying the warm sunshine.

Not yet did they know the feel of the hot branding iron or the sharp knife of the cowboy, yet they would. Leaving the head of Rawhide, we came out on a beautiful prairie; then, after some miles further along, we came to a wonderful stream known as Running Water. On the bank of this stream we found a road ranch where one could put up for the night or buy such supplies as were needed. One year later this ranch was moved down the creek one mile, and the place became known as Lusk,[1] named after a man who became my very good friend at a later period, Mr. Frank Lusk.

From Running Water our trail led due north for twelve miles over a flat tableland, as beautiful a piece of country as ever lay outdoors. After a long time we found ourselves seemingly on a bluff looking down into what is known as Hat Creek Basin,[2] famed as a most wonderful cow country.

North from our elevated position a wonderful panorama spread out as far as we could see and brought into display many of nature's wonderful creations. So spectacular was this view it made one feel glad he was allowed to see so much grandeur. Countless small hills dotted with countless cattle, horses, and other forms of life entered into the formation of this picture. Small streams with green trees fringing their banks went winding their crooked way to the north to join the parent stream, Lance Creek, and the Cheyenne River.

Presently we descended this long hill into the valley below, and after a tramp of four miles we arrived at Hat Creek Store,[3] or, as it was called, road ranch. For the next three years this place was to be my post office and depot of supplies, fifty miles from the home ranch. Reaching this ranch we made camp; although the hour was early, we desired above all things to sprawl out on our beds and rest.

As we thought of those long fifty miles to be traveled, we'd look at our tired and sore feet and groan. Mr. John Storey was owner of this ranch and store, and it was said he knew personally every cowpuncher who worked in that country and on what ranch he worked. This proved a convenience, as he knew exactly where to send out the mail or supplies. At this store a cowboy could purchase anything needed in his line with one notable exception: booze. This kind of merchandise was not kept in stock. However, we were not looking for such refreshments. Red meat and wholesome grub were the staples for us.

We had hardly become settled when here came Mr. Storey, and he instructed us that we could purchase anything he kept in stock without the cash, as Mr. Crawford had attended to the matter. This knowledge accelerated some movement among a few, as they needed tobacco, shirts, and other wearing apparel. None of the fellows seemed to care to loaf about the store, wasting good time that could be spent resting on their beds. All knew there were thirty long miles to knock off next day, and they must prepare for it the best they could.

Our slumbers were disturbed early next morning, as we must hustle around and get started on that long tramp to the ULA[4] ranch. After plenty of groaning and grumbling, we were on our way, yet we would take many short rests during the day, and at a late hour that evening we reached the ULA ranch on Lance Creek. To me it seemed I couldn't knock off another mile, and I'm sure all the others felt the same.

Thirty-five cowboys and a cook extended us a welcome that just naturally made us feel good. However, it was the cook that caused an acceleration of movement when he called "Chuck." He invited us to take seats at the long table in the mess room; then, assisted by numerous cowboys, the hot food was placed on the table, and we were told to fly at it.

Other ULA punchers cared for our work stock and stretched our tent, and by the time we finished the meal our camp was all fixed up for us. This cow ranch, like all other ranches, had its usual forms of entertainment such as cards, checkers, musical instruments, and, not the least, a set of boxing gloves, and at the conclusion of the meal we were invited to help ourselves.

Sam and I helped ourselves to a seat in a dark corner of the bunkroom, lit our pipes, and made the smoke fly. As Al entered the bunkroom, he spotted those boxing gloves, and in a few minutes he had everyone saying, "No, thank you." It was hard to feature anyone passing through all the grief we had the past nine days, without rest, wanting to have a bout with boxing gloves simply because there was a set of gloves handy. Yet Al did that very thing.

Naturally, all the ULA punchers turned him down, while our fellows did the same. It seemed no man wanted to be pounded up by that half-breed Indian, who looked amply qualified to do a good job of it. Seeing his chances to show off going glimmering, Al projected himself into our corner and invited Sam to go around.

"Gwan with yo ole fool boxing! Ah don't fight that way," declared Sam, and I noticed his hand drop down near his gun which he was wearing.

"You come and put them on, Kid. I won't slug you. We'll just tap lightly," said Al as he saw his last chance going glimmering.

"Nope! There's twenty long miles to knock off tomorrow. Nothing doing, Cowboy!" I told Al.

"Oh come on, Kid. Honest, I won't slug. Just for one round," pleaded Al.

"Say, you big stiff, pick on someone your size. You know very well there isn't room on the bed wagon for a cripple."

"Honest, Kid! You're not going to get hurt," continued Al, pleading.

"If you'd keep your word, one round wouldn't be so bad, but I'm so blooming tired. Yet I'm not afraid of you," and at the same time my hands were itching for the feel of those mitts.

"Come on and be a sport," and in another minute the gloves were tied on my hands, the bunkroom floor cleaned off in the center, and we were prancing around, trying to make ourselves believe we were the hot thing, when we should have been in our beds resting.

I soon had a hunch Al was going to pull something, and I was watching him close as we pesticated around in the room. All at once I saw a vicious gleam in Al's eyes, and I knew it was coming. It did come, and if Al had hit what he struck at, I would have ridden those twenty miles on the bed wagon. Fortunately for me, I was not in the range of that vicious lunge Al made at me, but as the momentum carried him by, his neck was terribly in the way of my fist as I threw my hundred and fifty pounds against it. Just now, things looked red, and that Indian took several of my best efforts before he recovered.

This ended the exhibition, and both sets of punchers were yelling themselves hoarse as all had heard him make a definite promise not to slug, and they seemed glad to see him take a trimming. Once more that old truth had been demonstrated, "When a fellow looks for something, he usually finds it."

During the hubbub that followed, Sam and I slipped out

of the ranch house and sought our beds in the tent, and the next thing I remember the cook was calling breakfast. Once more we had a fine meal with the ULA fellows. Then camp was cleaned up, and we started out on the last twenty miles of our long hike. The first ten miles were over a country the like of which I had never encountered before. It was a continuation of gullies, washouts, hogbacks, and small pinnacles, all as white as chalk, and not a green thing to be seen on that ten-mile stretch, with nary a drop of water to be found. The morning sun shining on the white surface proved hard on one's eyes, and it was a great relief when we left these badlands.

Now the country flattened out, and the green grass and grazing cattle were in abundance, which caused our minds to revert to our sore feet and tired bodies. The middle of the afternoon we came to the AU7 ranch, and our trials were over for the present. Practically, we were dead, but not buried; however, we would have been ready for that ordeal had we another day to tramp without rest.

Old Fred, the German cook at the ranch, knew better than any other man on the ranch how to bring back the smiles to our tired bunch. With some advance knowledge of the time of our arrival, he had his medicine all ready, and we had hardly seated ourselves when he yelled, "Chuck!"

Soon we tenderfeet learned that the word "chuck" would cause any hungry puncher to get on some movement quicker than a six-shooter. Fred piloted us into the mess room and, assisted by a bunch of punchers who had passed through a similar experience, proceeded to fill us up on a red-hot meal. After the meal we retired to the bunkroom, and it was at this time Mr. Crawford showed up long enough to get a count on us; then he faded from sight. We talked, smoked, and became acquainted, but finally our eyelids grew heavy; then we unrolled our beds and crawled into them.

On this ranch, Fred ruled the sun, moon, and stars, and when he yelled, every puncher must jump out and attend to the business in hand. However, on that particular morning his call was considerably delayed, and we were allowed to sleep late.

After a time we were called, and we enjoyed another of Fred's good meals, at the conclusion of which we retired to the bunkroom for our smoke and a general get-together. We were getting along famously when Sam upped and spilled the beans about our set-to at the ULA ranch. This gave me a notoriety I didn't like, but what could a fellow do about it? Well, I firmly resolved I'd never slip on the gloves again; yet in less than a week my face was sore as a boil, as I found some very clever boxers in the outfit.

Sam disappeared, and on looking him up I found him getting ready for the family washing. He had me spread our bedding out over the sagebrush to dry and bask in the sunshine until evening. Our soiled clothing was washed and boiled, then hung out on the sagebrush to dry.

With this job out of our way we had a wash in the river; then after shaving and getting into clean clothes, we not only looked better, but we felt a lot better.

---

[1]Originally a stage station serving traffic between Fort Laramie and the Black Hills. First known as Running Water, it became the town of Lusk in 1887 and was populated after that largely by grangers. See Osgood, p. 243; and *Wyoming: A Guide to Its History*, p. 224.

[2]One of the rich grazing areas north of the Platte River in Wyoming. S. F. Emmons' S-E cattle ranged there. See *Wyoming Stock Growers Association Brandbook*, p. 23, in *Cattleman's Frontier*.

[3]An historic spot on Highway 85 north of Lusk. It was originally founded by a small detachment of soldiers in 1868. Numerous stage hold-ups directed by Dunc Blackburn occurred near here. See *Wyoming: A Guide*, p. 223.

[4]Founded in 1880 and located on Lance Creek in Niobrara County about forty miles south of Hat Creek Station. John B. Kendrick himself helped fashion the logs and build the original house. Billy Keating, whom Mullins identifies as the foreman at the 4W Ranch, bought the ULA in the early 1890s. See *Pioneering on the Cheyenne River*, p. 6.

A Period of Depression

IT IS REMARKABLE how quickly a bunch of husky young men will snap back into life after enduring such a period of hardship as we did. Yet after a couple of days we were waiting our turn to slip on the gloves. At this ranch there were musical instruments galore, also cards, checkers, and other wholesome forms of amusement, yet there was no gambling.

We loafed and rested a week, and to have watched us go after the boxing gloves one would never believe we had been so near the borderline. It happened, while I was having a bout with the gloves, that Mr. Crawford stepped in and invited me to take a walk which ended at a small cabin near the stable.

"This is the shop I spoke of," said Jim. "Now, draft one, or every man on the ranch to help you, but get her going," and he pointed to a pile of junk we had bought in Cheyenne, which was lying on the floor. "It's the stuff you ordered."

Never would I have taken that nice little cabin for a blacksmith shop, as nothing indicated such but the junk on the floor. Sam, seeing Jim and me walking away from the crowd of almost forty men, had sensed trouble and followed us; he now stood grinning in the cabin door. At once I appointed him chief assistant, which brought a smile to Jim's face, and when that man smiled, it was worth seeing and would make a fellow feel good plumb down to his boots.

40

Sam was instructed to get busy, as business had commenced, and he hardly got started when here came the entire herd of punchers drilling to the shop. In a few minutes, I had a bunch of them rustling an anvil block, another digging a hole for it. Others were building a forge and hanging the bellows, while others were constructing a work bench. In twenty minutes there were more activities on that ranch than there had ever been. Jim was hopping around from one thing to another, making himself as useful as he could, while I had the satisfaction of bossing them. After a strenuous half-day's work, we were ready for the coal.

"That's easy," said Jim, and he started some men with a wagon to a crop in the river bank a mile from the ranch. After a time these boys returned with something that looked like coal. However, the smoke was different from any coal smoke I'd ever smelled. The coal gave off sparks to a degree; the shop was filled with them. The coal burned up completely, leaving no clinkers but instead disappearing in a white ash. To heat a piece of iron of small dimension was an impossibility, notwithstanding the bellows handle was worked to a frazzle.

"It's the coal," I told Jim. At once he sent the men to another crop for coal, but it proved to be the same kind and no good for our use. Jim had been working the bellows handle, and so strenuously had he worked, he was sweating something fierce. He had watched closely, and at the conclusion he wasn't only wet with sweat, but he was nervous and his face was black as a thundercloud. I thought he was thinking of the bag of coal I had marked on my list.

During the evening I had thought of a way around this tough luck, yet I said nothing about it until at the breakfast table. As we ate breakfast, Jim was in his usual place. However, I'll confess he wasn't looking happy, but rather as though he had had no sleep, for it was a long way to Cheyenne for just a sack of coal, and the blacksmith work couldn't go forward until we had it. Yes, Jim had a troubled look on his face and but very little to say, which naturally put a damper on the bunch, and all seemed depressed as there would be no roundup for our outfit until the blacksmith work had been done.

"While the work will go slow, I believe we can get by with charcoal," I remarked in a matter-of-fact way.

Heavens! what a reaction to those few words. Now Jim's face was wreathed in smiles, and even the boys snapped into life and commenced to joke.

At the conclusion of the meal Jim sent a number of men with two wagons and eight horses to a pine divide several miles from the ranch. When they returned, they had two large loads of dry cedar and pine logs. At the end of two weeks we had a stack of charcoal that resembled a small haystack and enough fuel to last a lifetime.

With our manufactured coal I started in on the work, the wagons coming first. Giving them the once-over, I thought they surely looked as though they needed a friend. Tires were wired on the felloes[1] of the wheels. Other parts were held together with rawhide thongs.

We started in on those tires, and while Sam wielded the sledge hammer, Jim usually pumped the bellows as he seemed interested in watching my work. This wagon work went slow as it took a long time to get a heat on iron with the charcoal, yet, like the traditional drop of water, under constant pressure the wagons gave way to the shoeing of the work horses. These in turn were followed by the mending of old broken branding irons and the making of new ones. With the branding irons out of the way, many other odd jobs requiring my attention were completed, and Jim confessed we were through blacksmithing for the present.

During this siege of work I commenced to learn this man Crawford and how he continually made his head work to keep us busy instead of allowing us to loaf around and get into trouble. Presently now, he had both wagons fitted out with two camp outfits; then, dividing the men, he sent us out over the range to place the branding pens in repair for the summer's work.

Sam and I drew the number that went along with Arch, Jim's brother, who took one outfit up Lodge Pole. This proved a dandy outing with nothing to do, only to feast our eyes on one of the finest cattle ranges in Wyoming.

Naturally, all the men except the cook rode horses, and this was the time I was to try out my new saddle, chaps, spurs, and high-heeled boots, as well as those old Colts I'd picked up in a secondhand store in Cheyenne. I suppose I must have felt much the same as those boys Sam and I had watched on the parade in Cheyenne.

Eight miles from the ranch we found our first branding pen, which needed one new post, a job one man could do in half an hour, yet we went into camp for the night. Sunup next morning found us trailing up Lodge Pole in search of the next pen. At this one, we found the gate needed slight attention, while one pole was absent, doubtless swiped by some cowboy, Indian, or trapper who needed a campfire. This job required a full day, and thus our caravan killed time until we reached the head of the creek.

Inasmuch as our labors had been so strenuous, Arch decided we'd go into camp and rest a couple of days before returning to the ranch. Whatever Arch said was law, so we camped and rested, at least the less ambitious fellows did. Having a nice fat, lazy bronc at my disposal, I decided to make a sightseeing trip. The summit of that high divide to the north was beckoning me to come and see what a beautiful picture Nature had to show me.

Having decided to go, I spoke of the trip to Sam, which met with violent opposition.

"You-all am gwan to go pesticating among dem rocks and get all smashed up, den who's gwan to help you," said Sam.

"Come on, Sam, the ride will do you good. You need the exercise; besides, we might see something interesting," but coax as much as I would, Sam couldn't be budged an inch from camp. Starting out alone, I made a trip that was to impress a picture on my mind I have never forgotten.

I had ridden almost four miles, constantly on the upgrade, until I came to the summit of the Belle Fourche divide.[2] There it was, spread out before me in any direction I wished to look, one of Nature's most beautiful pictures.

The panorama spread out into such vastness that it would challenge description, and only one other was I to see in Wyoming that proved as imposing. To me, it seemed impossible for mere man to paint on canvas even a fair imitation of this Nature picture as it stood out before me with all its colorings, its thousands of grazing cattle on a thousand hills, its numerous creeks, valleys, and tablelands.

After a mild winter, there came an early spring with its rains and warm sunshine which flooded the earth, causing it to take on a coating of green so restful to human eyes. Not only were there great herds of domesticated animals feeding on this nature food, placed there for that purpose, but there was wildlife in an abundance, perhaps uncountable creatures who, unseen by man, were feeding on nature's food, and to each there had been given intelligence sufficient to its needs.

Small streams fringed with cottonwood and box elder trees marked the course of the stream as it wended its way to the parent stream and disappeared on the horizon. Away over to the northeast rose a tower-like projection, seemingly out of the level prairie, to a height of many hundred feet. At a later date, I learned it was called the Devils Tower,[3] and up to that time in 1885 no man had ever climbed its perpendicular walls.

From my elevated position I looked to the east only to observe a black jagged line across the horizon, running from north to south and said to be the Black Hills. To the west the country flattened out into a vast prairie.

At this period, 1885, the great American bison had faded from the range, and the only evidences I saw while in Wyoming that the buffalo had ever existed were dead ones, rapidly fading into dust, or a pair of horns some puncher would occasionally find.

Sitting alone in silence on this high elevation, a sense of loneliness came over me; it seemed as if I might be in the presence of that Power that had created all, and that man was just an atom in the picture. I reasoned that some super intelligence had caused this complicated condition to come about, yet deluded man often questions the way of his Creator.

The man who says all this just happened to be as it is, and from age to age keeps happening with mathematical precision, should gaze on and study this picture. However, it matters but little what man thinks. We know we arrive on this earth in the form of flesh and molecular action. Here we remain until the purpose of our creation is served; then we go. Where to? None know further than that our bodies disintegrate into their chemical constituents, or elements, to form other compounds and create other elements that serve creation.

"Why, then," one might ask, "do we try to pry into the future life, when all has been prepared before we came, which is our Creator's way?"

With such weighty thoughts chasing one another through my mind, I filled the old pipe; then turning my horse about I cantered toward camp, leaving this picture behind. Yet in my mind it still remains, now forty-seven years later.

Riding into camp I found Sam all het up and nervous. He claimed he was getting ready to saddle a horse and hunt me.

"Wha am you all been, you fool kid? You all will sho want somebody to come heah, when you done get a nasty fall on some wild goose chase. Than wha is you?" he demanded to know.

The fact was, it had never occurred to me that I possibly could get a fall; my mind had been filled with more important things, and things I was never going to forget—the trip, the picture, and the lesson.

After another day we lined out for the ranch, and as we trailed along down Lodge Pole, I watched the calves frisk about their mothers in the warm sunshine, which caused me to wonder if some scientist would be able to tell where the T-bone came from when one of those calves had been served to him.

---

[1]The outside wooden rim of the wagon wheel, to which the steel tire is fitted and into which the spokes are inserted. See M. T. Richardson, ed. *Practical Blacksmithing,* 4 vols. in 1, 1889, 1890, 1891, rpt. (New York: Weathervane Books, 1978, vol. 4), p. 100.

[2]A divide created by the Belle Fourche River running through northeastern Wyoming by Devils Tower and then into South Dakota.

[3]A famous landmark near the Belle Fourche River in Crook County, northeastern Wyoming, twenty-eight miles northwest of Sundance. The nation's first national monument, Devils Tower is a huge column of fluted volcanic stone rising 1,280 feet into the air.

Working the Town Herd

AFTER LANDING AT the ranch from the excursion up Lodge Pole, we found Jim hadn't thought of a thing in the way of work, so we were doomed to eating, sleeping, and monkeying around the ranch, which soon got under our skins. We decided some excitement must be created, or there might be murder committed.

At this time one of the older and more experienced men came to the rescue by suggesting we work the town herd, and it was decided to do so after breakfast next morning. The town herd was made up of a dozen, more or less, mixed cattle that loafed about the stable through the winter months, grabbing off any spear of hay thrown out of the stable. In this way the town herd went through the winter, keeping reasonably fat.

The town herd served two useful purposes. First they furnished us with reasonable beef fat during the lean months. Second, they contributed to the punchers' entertainment on certain occasions and were about to do so now. After the morning meal the entire population of the ranch retired to the corral about the stable where the town herd was found busily engaged on the manure pile, none realizing the calamity hanging over them.

The corral gate was closed while two punchers saddled horses, after which the stable door was tightly closed and the

door latched. All being in readiness, the two punchers roped
the largest steer by the horns and the hind feet; then in a
second he was stretched out on the ground, after which a
short rope was made fast about his middle.

All of the gang were lined up on the fence, and now a
yell went up for a rider. After considerable persuasion a long-
legged puncher slid off the fence, buckled on a pair of spurs,
jumped astride the steer, and instructed the ropers to "Let
him go." Go was right, as the steer leaped into the air so
high he could look over the corral fence. When the steer hit
the ground, his legs were as stiff as fence posts, which caused
the rider to receive an awful jolt. Up and down, round and
round went the steer, the puncher clinging to his rope for
dear life.

To add to our entertainment, the steer gave off a roar
each time he hit the ground, yet it didn't faze the puncher. I
thought it marvelous how fast that steer could work as he
jumped and twisted, trying to unseat the rider. Finally, however, the steer ran short on wind or else decided it couldn't
be done, so he eased up and would only stand and kick at
the puncher's spurs. The entire population was on top of the
fence, shouting words of encouragement to the rider. However, he needed no encouragement as he was a capable rider.
The steer having surrendered, the puncher slid from his back
and made a quick run for the fence as he had no desire to
have those sharp horns stuck into him.

The next victim to receive attention was the large old
bull. He stood with the other cattle in the corral corner watching the Wild West performance, seemingly deeply interested.
Perhaps he was thinking his turn would come next, and it
did. After the bull was roped and stretched out ready for a
rider, a call went up for Sam Mathers. In a loud voice Sam
protested riding bulls.

"Ah's gwan git all de bucking I wants on de roundup.
Ain't gwine ride no bull, nohow," he declared. I had a hunch
that Sam just wanted to be coaxed and was itching to jump

astride of the bull. The call for Sam became so loud and insistent that he was obliged to come through. With much rumbling and grumbling the old boy slid off the fence and buckled on his spurs, all the while abusing crazy cowpunchers about riding bulls. In another minute he jumped astride of the bull and took a firm hold on the rope. The bull was cut loose and the big show was on.

With a roar of rage the bull leaped to his feet, and upon finding he had a passenger aboard, things happened so fast I almost lost track of events. The first leap took them up in the tree tops, and they hit the ground like a charge of dynamite. The ground trembled, and the corral fence rattled. It looked like no man could long survive such jolts, yet Sam hung onto his rope and his smile. In the meantime he was working his spurs on the bull's sides till they turned red, and likewise made the bull see red.

The mad bull started on a run for the corral fence as though he'd smash through it. This caused a quick scattering of the punchers located on top of the rail. Just before the bull reached the fence, he had a change of mind and, planting both feet in the ground, whirled so quickly it was all Samuel could do to keep from going right on over the fence. Yet Sam stuck to him, still smiling, and soon the bull stopped bucking and stood kicking sullenly at the spurs still raking his sides. Sam understood he had the bull whipped and that the time had come for him to make his getaway from the animal. This is a dangerous move, which all punchers know, as the animal usually turns in pursuit and tries to rip the puncher with his sharp horns. Sam watched his chance, jumped from the bull's back, and hotfooted it for the fence, arriving safely.

A long yearling is an overgrown calf that has shed its mother and gone out in the world on its own hook, and the town herd membership included a few of these prodigal sons. Quickly one of these yearlings was stretched on the ground ready to contribute its mite to our entertainment.

This time the call went up for Jimmy Tuff,[1] a short, blocky boy of Jewish extraction, whose real name was William Gabriel and who hailed from New York City. Jimmy was a clever boy, always brimful of deviltry, and counted every man in the outfit his friend. Jimmy had short, stubby legs, yet they could stick to a bronc like the tentacles of an octopus. Of course, Jimmy protested riding yearlings, but after a due process of coaxing, he straddled the yearling, and the boys cut it loose. Some fast work followed, and in less than half a minute Jimmy hit the ground, nothing hurt but his dignity. Jimmy demanded another trial but no use; Jimmy couldn't stick the yearling, and the calf was duly christened the champion outlaw.

Now the gates were opened and the town herd scooted for the big open spaces, not to be seen again until fall when the grass became short and scarce; then back they came again to take their respective places on the manure pile, where no particle of hay could escape them. This ended the show for this spring, and while we had a jolly good time and laughed ourselves sick, we soon forgot the day's sport as more important matters came up almost at once to engage our serious attention. There was from now on an entire change of program.

A string of horses in a cow outfit in those days consisted of five to eight head of saddle horses to a man. Each horse in the outfit had its own individual name, which was known to all the older riders. In this outfit the number was six head to the man, and he must so regulate the riding of them that all would remain in about the same condition. No man must ride another's horse unless by special permission from the owner; otherwise, it was cause for serious trouble.

In the horse herd, something over two hundred and fifty head of saddle horses, there were a number of outlaws, a few locoed animals, some old and unfitted for use, and some crippled ones. Yet all those horses were to be ridden by someone, and it was this very thing that caused a lot of worry for the older punchers as none of them desired to ride the outlaws or locoed horses, while every man wanted very much to ride the good circle and cow horses.

Just who the lucky or unlucky riders were to be no one in the outfit knew just yet but Mr. Crawford, and I'll confess some of the older punchers couldn't sleep well until after the parceling of the horses. Personally, all of the horses looked good to me, but I would be wiser next year.

A few days after the Wild West performance the horses were run into the corral at the ranch, all of them kicking up their heels and rolling in fat. However, six weeks later these same horses wouldn't be so frisky and not a buck left in any of them. I knew there were six head in that bunch that would be my very own, and I gazed on the herd with considerable pride. But wait; I was to find that all that glittered wasn't gold.

Jim and Arch, with ropes in hand, entered the corral while all the punchers lined up on top of the fence with their ropes in readiness. Catching a horse, they'd call some puncher's name; then he'd slide off the fence, place his rope on the horse, and lead him from the corral. Each man must accept the horse given him and no back talk about it. Should some fellow refuse to ride some particular horse, he must leave the outfit and seek work elsewhere. Yet if he did so, he would run into the same conditions elsewhere.

Having been previously instructed, I took pencil and paper, and thereon I made notations of the names of the horses which I drew. This would keep me from making any mistake in roping out a horse until such time as I became acquainted with my horses. I would ask Harry Crain,[2] our wrangler, to point out the horse I wanted; then I would try to rope him. My string certainly looked good to me, and I had a feeling of pride as I led each horse from the corral—but wait a while.

On drawing some horses a puncher would turn pale and say things in a low voice so the boss couldn't hear him as he discovered he had drawn an outlaw or a locoed horse. A locoed horse was one that had gone crazy from eating loco weed and was apt to throw his head up in the air and start running no matter where, over an embankment perhaps. However, I never heard of anyone being seriously hurt by a locoed horse.

The parceling over, we made haste to get ready for the roundup. These preparations included laundering, mending, haircutting, shaving, airing beds—in fact a thousand things had to be done before we headed out for the big adventure.

---

[1]Not the only example of Jimmy Tuff's endurance and skill. An example of Tuff's hardiness is found in an incident in 1897, when he and his brother, Bert, rode two mustang horses from near Sheridan to Galena, Illinois, to prove the hardiness of these animals. See *The Trampling Herd*, p. 268.

[2]Later a prominent Wyoming legislator. In 1923, a collection of letters written at Crain's request was published in a volume entitled *Letters from Old Friends and Members of the Wyoming Stock Growers Association* (Cheyenne: S. A. Bristol Company, 1923). These letters, dated 1915, recount much of the early history of Wyoming's livestock industry.

A Hot Footrace

THE GENERAL ROUNDUP was the one large event of the year, and during this year it proved to be the largest roundup ever held in Wyoming, covering more country and rounding up more cattle than ever was done before or since. Every cow outfit in the country participated in this roundup, and all were going on at the same time, only each roundup covered a different section of country. These general roundups usually started about the fifth of June as by this time both cattle and horses had come back from a long winter and were in splendid condition.

When once started, these roundups were continuous, usually lasting six weeks or until a definite country had been covered and all cattle that had drifted from their home range during the winter had been returned to their range. Naturally, the drift during the winter was southeast, and it would be south of a home range that the outfits would find their hard work.

A representative, or rep, as used in cowpuncher language, is a top puncher, one qualified to look after his outfit's interest on any roundup. The home outfit will work south of their range, then send reps to neighboring outfits that they may gather any of their outfit's cattle found on the roundup they attend and at the conclusion of the roundup drive the cattle found to the home range before

53

joining their own outfit. These reps are supposed to know all brands in their immediate country and where and to whom they belong, even though the cattle have long hair and the brand is difficult to figure out. It was an unwritten law that all reps should see to it that cattle adjacent to their home range should be returned home if found on the roundup they attend.

These reps, on leaving the home wagon or outfit, would cut out their strings of horses, then pack their beds on them and drive to the distant roundup where they would put in with some outfit and work as that outfit's men. It was the rep's business to look through every bunch of cattle driven on the roundup ground, and should he find any of his brand, or that of his neighbors, he would cut them into the herd where they were held until the roundup was over. Then he would cut out his cattle, drive them to the home range, and turn them loose.

Often a flock of reps from the same country attending a roundup worked together, which facilitated and made their job easy. While working with an outfit, a rep must do all the work the same as a regular puncher, with the exception that he never stood day herd when a roundup was in operation.

Those last few days at the ranch were busy ones for all, and when all were ready to go, the boys looked a very clean and respectable bunch of young men. However, I will hesitate long enough to say our fellows had no resemblance to the cowboys pictured in the movies, which is something to be thankful for. Presently we were ready for the big adventure. Then one morning early, Fred let out a whoop that caused all hands to throw back their tarpaulins and roll out and into their clothes. Each man rolled and tied his bed into a compact roll, then tossed it on the bed wagon. With this chore finished, we filled up on Fred's chow; then the work stock were caught, harnessed, and hitched to the wagons. We next caught saddle horses and saddled them, and we were all set for the trail. However, a short wait was necessary as the OS fellows had not arrived.

This OS² outfit had their ranch five miles up the Cheyenne River from the AU7, and both outfits used practically the same range; consequently, the wagons worked together all through the roundup season as one outfit. Shortly the OS outfit came; then everything mixed except the horses, and they rubbered at each other from the distance.

To me, it was an inspiring sight to watch that large caravan of cowboys, horses, and wagons drilling down the trail toward the roundup ground almost thirty miles distant. There were fully eighty cowboys, counting the reps that had put in with us, and it seemed that they rode mostly in pairs while all were perfectly busy with their chatter. At noon we went into camp near the old Bridle Bit² Ranch. Here we had our dinner and whiled away another hour, then perambulated down the river to the mouth of Lance Creek near the 9 9 9 Ranch. It was found that several outfits had beat us there, and there was a number still to come. However, we were to rest a day or two before starting work.

This arrangement gave us a lot of idle time we had no use for, so some form of entertainment must be inaugurated and the Indian was the answer. For some time past, Al had made it known that he was something of a sprinter, and I'll confess the boy did look like he could run like a scared hound. It just naturally looked like Al could step along to the time of ten seconds; at least he had most of the punchers believing he could. He even looked good to the OS boys who hadn't heard of his boxing experience.

Just to see Al dressed up in that beautiful brown skin and white teeth, with large humps of muscle standing out in wads all over his body, would convince the most skeptical that he could step off fast. One thing sure—he enjoyed having the boys admire his beautiful form as he pranced through the various camps.

Scouting around through the various camps for a racer,

a small, skinny individual was located in the 9 9 9 camp. The 9 9 9 fellows thought their man could run a bit, in fact about eight dollars' worth, which was all the money that could be rustled in our two outfits.

With the bets made and the plans for the race completed, it was surprising how Al snapped back, and once more he became the big chief. Presently Al had all the fellows eating out of his hand. Even Curtis Spaugh, the OS foreman, and Mr. Crawford were wild about Al, and after all arrangements were made, they took personal charge of him. They saw that his muscles were massaged by the hour, using lard borrowed from Fred for the purpose.

Things just looked too bad for the little 9 9 9 horse wrangler, yet his backers would insist they still had a few dollars they'd be glad to stake on their man.

Sam and I made a trip to the 9 9 9 camp so that we could see first-hand what Al was up against. One look was sufficient, and it would cause even a skeptic to place his bets on the Indian. We were filled with gloom as we wanted to see the Indian skinned alive. To us, the skinny, tubercular-looking individual looked as though he should be in Arizona rusticating on cactus instead of running footraces and wrangling horses at night.

In our camp it would have been treason to say one disrespectful word about Al, so we kept quiet and let Nature take its course. Years later, while working over a skinny subject in the dissecting room, I thought of this footrace and of Al and what a wonderful service he would serve if I had him on the table before me. Yet that perfect anatomical specimen would prance through life serving no useful purpose, and I thought that a pity.

Pandemonium prevailed in all camps, except the 9 9 9. Here the boys claimed they still had a few shekels they would gladly bet on their man. In our camp and that of the OS, every white dime had been contributed to the fund. Of course Sam and I had a good alibi as we hadn't a nickel left; besides, I remembered my vow in the Gold Room not to bet.

The time set for the race was at hand, and every man on the roundup was on his toes impatiently waiting for the race to start. Quickly now the Indian pranced out on the course, dressed up in that brown skin with a fresh coat of lard and those beautiful white teeth, which he constantly showed.

If Al could have crossed the divide at this time it would have been the thing to do as this man was at the supreme achievement of his short life. Without doubt the Great Spirit would have handed him a choice seat in his special Wigwam, there to bask in the sunshine of his smiles through all the time to come. Yet it was not to be. In a few minutes Al would be the most humiliated Indian that ever followed a blind trail.

The conquering chief pranced into position with eyes sparkling, chest bulging, and head thrown back with every white tooth showing. In his hand he clutched two sagebrush twigs, while that yellow hide glistened in the sunshine like gold. Never for a moment did he glance at the poor, skinny form that meekly stood at his side waiting the signal to go. It seemed no pair of eyes could stray further than the wonderful form of the Indian, on which humps of muscle stood out like mountains in a desert.

The pistol was fired and they were off, while every cowboy held his breath and watched, fully expecting to see the Indian leap ahead and lose the little night wrangler. Yet all were disappointed as it was the little wrangler who leaped ahead of the Indian and ran off and lost him.

Al, seeing no hope of ever beating him out, slowed down to a trot, circled the crowd, and went to camp and into a tent, the most despised man on the roundup. The little streak of lightning had caused the punchers to lose their money, yet he was warmly congratulated and he became the roundup hero.

"He shore runs just lak he-all boxed," said Sam [of the Indian] as we walked back to camp.

As I have said, Jim's face was expressive, and at this time he looked like he had murder in his heart as he thought of what Al had done to the punchers. It wasn't so much for the kale the outfit lost on Al, but it was the humiliation of a misplaced confidence, and it meant plenty of trouble for Al. That same evening, to the surprise of the punchers, Al took the horses out in the hills and wrangled them all through the night with howling coyotes for company.

While in camp, the punchers made life perfectly miserable for Al. They would discuss racing and boxing in all their various forms, yet no direct conversation was had with Al, and I had a notion it was a shabby thing to do. Al had honestly thought he could deliver the goods, and he must have a try, even though he lost.

Anyway, Al had had a good time while it lasted; but now he was paying, as night wrangling is the most despised job on a roundup, and no self-respecting puncher will follow it for any extended time. Some days later when we came in from a drive and went to camp for a change of horses, Fred told us Al had gone—the Devil knew where; he didn't.

---

[1]Owned by the Union Cattle Company with Thomas Sturgis as president. The OS Ranch was located near the confluence of Black Thunder Creek and the Cheyenne River. In 1888, the Union Cattle Company declared insolvency but continued to operate for many years thereafter. See *Pioneering on the Cheyenne River*, p. 5.

[2]Owned by the Union Cattle Company with Thomas Sturgis as president. The Bridle Bit Ranch was built in "1878 on the Cheyenne River, four miles west of the junction of Lance Creek." See *Pioneering on the Cheyenne River*, p. 5.

A Slow Race

WITH ANOTHER IDLE day on our hands, something must be done to dispel the gloom or murder might be committed, and that wouldn't do at all. Sam in his nonchalant way remarked, "We-all mout have a slow race." Those seven words went through the camp like an electrical spark and penetrated to all the other camps, acting on the punchers like magic. Everyone snapped back into good humor. One of those smiles reached even Jim's face; then he couldn't do anything but smile as he knew just what was going to happen and that he would be one of the chief actors.

I was green regarding slow races, but I had a receptive mind and consulted my book of knowledge. I asked Sam for enlightenment on slow races.

"A slow race am a race wha I done ride your mule, and you-all done ride my mule; don we'll see who-all am gwan to get out fust. It sho am heaps of fun," declared Sam with a grin on his face. During those far off days in cow outfits, most every horse herd had a mascot, usually a small mule or burro which served no useful purpose other than entertainment. An outfit would bet their mascot was the slowest of any on the roundup. Every outfit would enter their racer, but it must be ridden by the foreman of another outfit, who would lambast the life out of it, trying to get through first.

I asked myself, after learning all the facts about slow races, just what Jim would do with those long legs of his. However, I had an idea he'd fold them up about the horn of the saddle and probably get along very nicely.

When the small beasts were dressed with those large cowboy saddles and bridles, no part of the mule was exposed but head, ears, tail, and hoofs. The fact was the mules looked uncanny, and had I met one while alone out in the hills, I probably would have been running yet. When all these mascots were lined up ready for their riders, they presented quite a front, even though they were a queer-looking conglomeration.

The time came for Jim to mount, and he separated his legs and walked over to his mount and sat down in the saddle. But those legs would surely drag along on the sagebrush, and if his mule started going, he'd be obliged to fold them up. After a lot of jocularity by that large gathering of cowboys, the mules and their riders were in position, ready for the crack of the pistol.

The pistol was fired, and the racers were supposed to be off on the run; however, nothing of the kind occurred. Those small runts just stood quietly with a pathetic look in their eyes, enough to make an angel weep, and they utterly refused to budge an inch. Spurring was impossible, there being no exposed surface. Quirting was confined to the ears and tail, and it did not cause them to move; they stood batting their eyes and waiting. After many repeated efforts trying to move them, the riders drew their pistols, firing them close to the mules' hind feet, but it did no good.

In a few instances the mules did advance a few steps, then came to a halt and waited for the next bombardment. In no possible way could those riders make their mounts travel, as they were stubborn little fellows, and that race was never finished.

That large bunch of cowpunchers went wild, and they said enough rotten things to those riders to have caused a shooting match at any other time. Yet there was a lot of fun and no sore spots left after it was over; besides, it drove away the gloom resulting from the fast race.

Now, after a period of forty-seven years, the picture remains as clear in my mind as it was on the day the race wasn't run. Al did not have the nerve to show up at the slow race but remained rolled up in his blankets. Soon the day was gone, and good feeling had been restored. Next morning at three a show would start that was going to last six long weeks, and there would be no intermission. At its finish, we would be soiled, bewhiskered, and tired while some of us were going to be considerably wiser.

"Roll out for chuck!" came the big noise next morning at three; then the flaps of forty tarpaulins were thrown back, and forty cowpunchers jumped out and dressed. Right then things commenced to move, and it was whiz-bang for six weeks or the duration of the roundup.

Ten minutes later the meal was finished, and the boys with rope in hand were circling around the horse herd, trying to rope out their mounts. Al had prepared a temporary corral by tying the ends of two long ropes to the wheels of the bed wagons while two punchers swung on to the other ends, forming a V-shaped space for the horses.

Our day wrangler, Harry E. Crain, was first to rope out his mount and relieve Al, who rolled up in his blankets. It was at this time we tenderfeet were having the biggest trouble of our young lives, trying to rope the particular horses we had selected to ride this morning. I had planned to ride old Blue, but it seemed impossible to locate him; then Harry pointed the horse out, but to get my rope on his neck without getting several other necks in the loop was an impossibility for me at this time. However, being strong on trying to do things on my own hook, I threw the loop several times with negative results. Sam saw what a predicament I was in and came to my rescue. The first throw of Sam's caught Blue, and I led him from the herd.

I found Harry E. Crain, our day wrangler, a prince of a

Cowboys on Powder River in Wyoming during the open range period that Mullins writes about. *Photo courtesy American Heritage Center, University of Wyoming.*

boy despite the fact he was born in Vermont and educated in Boston. Harry was the owner of a ravenous appetite, and he always had it with him. He loved beans, and it mattered little to him whether they were freshly cooked or a trifle sour. All alike were good eating for Harry. In addition to his many excellent qualities, he was the best horse wrangler that ever threw his leg over a bronc. During my three years in close association with him, I never knew a time when he had enough to eat; and whenever not busy with his horses, he could be found rustling in some camp for food. Harry had a speaking acquaintance with every cook on the roundup, and believe me, those cooks had plenty of fun feeding him.

Harry was a rapid talker, especially when in argument over some disputed point, and I found it difficult to follow him. Yet, while he did talk fast, he talked sense, a thing some punchers were incapable of doing. Forty-three years after leaving the AU7 outfit, I attended the Frontier Days in Cheyenne and made a visit to Harry's palatial home. For two short hours we visited, yet he was the same old scout and insisted on doing all the talking.

On this first morning every man selected his best circle horse, my selection being old Blue whom Sam had roped for me. Had I not been so busy with my saddling of Blue, I might have noticed the older punchers smiling and winking at each other as they watched me. Blue was rollicky and fat, and on this particular morning he decided to show me what he could do in the way of bucking. However, it would have been better for Blue had he been a good horse that morning.

On mounting him, he started right into bucking, but his effort was crowhopping in a straight line and without frills. Quickly I found I could sit him straight up and without pulling leather. The results of this experience caused Blue to buck almost every time I rode him. After Blue had his fun, he quieted and was a good, faithful, old horse, and now that he was through, I had time to look about and observe what the other horses were doing. At my first count I was able to count ten riderless horses scooting over the prairie with punchers in hot pursuit.

After a time the horses were restored to their riders, and quiet prevailed. We rode out to the top of a small hill, where the cowboys gathered. Looking over this large bunch of men, mostly young, I thought them the pick of America's young manhood, and there must have been over three hundred. I was proud to be associated with them.

I was soon to learn that many of these men passed under an alias, such as Chuck, Shorty, Speck, Windy, Shanks, Red, and dozens of other names, and for many of them I never learned any other name. Where there were two or more with the same alias on a roundup, one would be known as AU7 Chuck or Shorty.

By some stroke of fortune Mr. Crawford, our boss, happened to be roundup foreman, and he bossed the roundup. Quickly Jim started the wheels or horses to moving by sending out the drives. That the reader may have a clear conception of a drive, and how clean the cattle can be combed out of a country, we will follow out one drive to a finish as all drives are about the same.

My First General Roundup

M R. CRAWFORD ORDERED Curt Spaugh,[1] the OS foreman, to take forty men up the river and drive out that
country. Another foreman he ordered to take a similar number and go down the river and drive up. Still another foreman
he ordered to take seventy men and drive Lance Creek. Presently all those men were racing in different directions over
the country, leaving only the roundup foreman on the ground.

When all these men were properly distributed, there would
be a cordon of men around a section of country twenty-five
miles across in any direction, from which nothing could escape being driven in. Old Blue and I managed to get off with
Curt Spaugh's drive, but to keep up with him and the
procession—well, that's another story. Curt looked like a
mighty intelligent fellow, but when he lit out on a keen run
and kept it up for twelve miles, I wasn't so sure but what he
was nutty.

While the hoard of cowboys were at his heels at the start,
many dropped back for the simple reason that their horses
couldn't keep up. On and on that wild cowboy flew over the
country, sagebrush flats, ditches, prairie dog towns, up and
down hill, never slackening his speed, and I thought most of
the men were doomed for a tumble.

Blue and I experienced plenty of trouble trying to keep
in sight of the racing cowboys, but despite our best efforts

we constantly dropped behind, notwithstanding Blue was doing his best, aided by my sharp spurs. Blue's sides were turning red, due to the jabs I constantly gave him as I feared I'd lose the gang. Despite our best efforts, we were a mile behind at the finish.

Presently I came up to the cowboys, who had all dismounted and were taking a smoke while the horses were getting their second wind. I'll admit I was short on experience, as I'd hardly started to learn. Just the same I dismounted and lit my pipe. This halt was just the customary thing, as the horses must rest and be recinched, ready for the second spasm.

Taking a look at Blue's cinch, I found it hung an inch from his belly, and it was a wonder the saddle hadn't turned with me. I noticed Curt give Blue a caustic look; then he quietly told me to remain with him as my horse might set me afoot out in the hills trying to follow those crazy punchers.

Of course I was green, but I was going to be much wiser before we reached camp, and as I knew Curt was boss, I did as he told me to. All being rested and recinched, the second spasm was started by sending an older puncher with fifteen men to the south divide while another took the same amount of men and lit out for the north divide, the remainder of the bunch remaining right there until the cattle commenced to come into the river bottom.

The leader to the south divide lit out on the run for the divide, riding as straight as he could, and every little while he dropped off a man who remained right there until the cattle commenced coming down off the divide. This continued until they reached the divide, where contact was made with the men driving Lance Creek. The leaders headed down the divide, turning every cow either toward the river or Lance Creek.

As these cattle commenced coming off the divide, the men dropped off would pick them up and push them along to the next man, who would shove them on. Presently a line of cattle extending from the divide to the river were coming in. At this time Curt and his bunch of men commenced to gather the cattle from both sides of the river and to drive toward the roundup ground.

There were many young calves coming in with the cattle, and before we had driven five miles, we had hundreds of cows and calves milling amongst the drags.[2] Soon the calves became lost from their mothers in this milling mass, which caused a fearful mess. As we progressed, the herd became larger every moment, while the dust kicked up by the slowly moving herd hung like a thick fog over all alike.

By this time Old Sol had risen in the sky, and the higher it rose, the hotter it became, causing every man to strip almost to the skin and tie his garments on his saddle. As we continued progressing, our herd grew larger, the dust thicker, and the heat more fearful. It became so hot it seemed that blisters would be burned on our backs, yet we must continue punching cows and calves toward the roundup ground, regardless of personal suffering from heat and thirst.

There were hundreds of calves, and each calf had a mother from which it had become separated, which created a condition of milling and bawling hard to overcome. The old cows would mill through the drags smelling each calf, each hoping to find her own, while each calf would hustle around hunting its mother, but to find each other—well, it couldn't be done.

Naturally this mixture made up the drags, and driving them was the place where the tenderfeet earned their thirty-five per month. Calves would break out of the herd and run back, thinking perhaps their mothers were behind; then some puncher would have a fast race. At times a cowboy would be obliged to rope and drag a calf back to the herd, no matter if it did scrape the skin from its sides on the sagebrush and cactus.

Experienced punchers would loosen their slickers and ride back and forth behind the herd shaking them, which stimulated the calves to move on. Other punchers would make small loops in their ropes and practice heel roping. These ropers had two objects in view—it stimulated the calves to move on, and it gave them needed practice at heel roping.

When we were obliged to cross a stream of water, the leaders wouldn't stop to take a drink, even though they were famished with thirst. Plunging into the stream they would poke their heads up and start upstream, and it seemed an impossible task to stop them. To do so, the older men would get in front of them and fire their pistols near their noses, which usually had the desired effect.

As our herd moved toward the roundup on this first drive, we were famished with thirst, yet we dared not leave the herd to hunt a drink of water. This experience proved romantic in the extreme, and very different from those of the cowboys pictured on movie screens of today. Often while watching such productions screened as are now produced of cowboys, I wonder if the writer ever saw fifty head of cattle together in one bunch.

Before reaching the roundup ground with our herd, I had nearly resolved to jump my job, as there were a lot of things I'd rather do than to punch drags along over a dusty, hot trail. As our herd neared camp, the circle contracted, and presently all the men were with the cattle. Eventually we drove our herd onto the roundup ground, and after Mr. Crawford showed us where he wished the herd placed, we scooted for our camp as fast as our tired horses would go.

What was true of this drive was, in a general way, true of all the others, and by the time all the drives were in, there must have been over eight thousand cattle on the roundup ground.

On reaching camp, it was remarkable how quickly the punchers hit the ground and unsaddled their horses. With equal alacrity the boys gulped down quarts of water, trying to quench their thirsts. No time was lost in filling our tin plates out of those Dutch ovens which were full of red-hot food. It was an unwritten law that this meal must be eaten in a hurry, as there were hungry and thirsty men holding the cattle who had a great desire to be relieved. As soon as a man finished eating, he grabbed his rope and caught his saddle horse, then away to the herd, and what a joy to those punchers left with the cattle to see him coming!

In the fewest possible minutes those thirsty and hungry punchers were in camp putting away that belated meal while other punchers were catching out their fresh horses and saddling them so that no time would be lost. Reaching the herds, it was found that Jim had reserved two bunches of cattle for our two outfits to start in on. The cattle from both herds were cut into one bunch, which facilitated the work all through the roundup.

The cows and calves were cut out first; then the dry stock were cleaned out, and after the reps looked through the herds, we were ready for the next bunch. In this way the work went forward until every herd in the roundup had been worked; then, after a change to fresh horses, boys in sufficient numbers were sent to drive our starting herd to the next roundup ground, perhaps twenty miles away.

Harry had his horses conveniently close at the end of the work; then all hands caught out their road horses and jollied along to the next campground while some would help Harry drive his herd of horses. Long ago, Fred had broken camp and driven to the next one, and by this time he would be preparing supper.

Notwithstanding that we were all shot when we got in off that first drive, I was to learn that plenty of water and a good meal under our belts did more to cause a comeback, especially when mounted on a fresh horse, than any other thing.

Jim, acting as roundup foreman, had no time to run his own cow outfit, so this part was turned over to his brother, Arch, who was a splendid cowman. What our outfit did was duplicated by all the outfits, and when all were finished, the remaining cattle were left on the ground to drift wheresoever they wished.

On reaching the new camp, the punchers had no time to flop down on their beds and rest, for after eating supper they must catch their night horses, and several of them would trail back to meet the herd and relieve those men. As the shades of evening covered the earth, our herd was rounded in on a level piece of ground near camp and held there until morning. To hold the cattle, men in sufficient number were named to stand the four reliefs and hold the cattle on the bed ground. Reliefs were divided into four periods; the first went on after supper and stood until ten, the second went out at ten and stood until twelve, while the last relief herded the cattle from two until relieved by the day herders.

After a riper experience, I learned that singing was an important factor in keeping the cattle quiet. It mattered little what the song or tune was, just so long as it was kept going. It seemed there was something about the noise the punchers called singing that had a soothing influence on the cattle's nerves. Especially was this true with beef cattle. It seemed that this class of cattle just loved the vocal efforts of the punchers. Often I have seen, while on night guard, that if the boys let up on the singing or mumbling, then some old beef steer would rise to his feet and turn around a time or two, and, if the singing was resumed, he'd lie down.[3] On the other hand, if the singing wasn't resumed, that same steer might give a snort and as quick as lightning the entire herd would be on their feet and racing over the country in what tenderfeet called a stampede.

At first it seemed to me the singing was more for the purpose of keeping the puncher awake than of keeping the cattle quiet; yet, with a riper experience, I found this was not true, as our vocal efforts really had a quieting influence on the cattle.

The hours for work on a roundup were rotten: from three in the morning until we could roll up in our blankets of an evening, then two hours for night guard between times. With this loss of sleep, it is a wonder we could possibly keep awake.

Standing night guard was where a well-trained horse came in handy. With such a horse one could train himself to sleep holding on to the saddle horn, while the horse trotted around the herd. A puncher knowing the capabilities of his horse could rest assured the horse would see any animal leaving the herd, and he would be right after him without orders from the rider.

After having trained myself to put on this stunt, I have all but had my neck unjointed by my horse giving a sudden spring after some absconding cow or steer. During black stormy nights, night guard was hazardous, as a good night horse cared nothing about the darkness or the contour of the ground when he saw some cow leaving the herd, and he would be cut off like a pistol ball.

---

[1]Foreman of the OS Ranch and brother of Addison Spaugh. Curtis is mentioned in a novel by Frazier Hunt, *The Long Trail From Texas*. The novel, first published serially under the title *The Last Frontier*, is subtitled *The Story of Ad Spaugh* (New York: Doubleday, Doran, and Company, 1940).

[2]Cattle which congregate at the rear of the herd because of weak condition or other factors.

[3]Apparently a common practice. There is considerable argument over the reason for and effect of the cowboys' singing to the cattle. This comment by Mullins tends to support the sometimes belittled notion that the sound of the singing served to calm the livestock.

One Tough Drive

O N THE SECOND MORNING of this roundup, Arch named me as one to go on day herd. This meant I should hurry out to the herd and relieve the last guard, then remain with the cattle until relieved, no matter when. Shortly I was to learn that day herd was a despised job, and if followed for three days, the puncher usually chucked up his job. I also learned that should a foreman desire to can a puncher, and do it without pain, he'd put him on day herd and keep him there until he quit. It took three days, usually. I learned that day herd had curative values that were more effective than medicine. Should some puncher claim to be sick, he was promptly placed on day herd, and there he remained until he confessed he was well. However, I saw a few cases where this treatment failed, much to the chagrin of the foreman.

Having received sentence to go on herd, I caught and saddled my horse, then went to the relief of the last guard. Now it was our business to graze our herd out into the hills and hold them until they became thirsty; then we would throw them on water where they would drink their fill and lie around for a couple of hours.

While grazing, the herd of cattle would become scattered; then we would park ourselves on some convenient hilltop, overlooking the herd at different points about them, and try to keep awake. Our work now consisted in seeing that none of the cattle should stray away, and to do this successfully without dozing was hardly possible. We understood that to be caught sleeping by a boss while on day herd was an unpardonable sin, and it might cause a puncher to lose his job. So far as the punchers were concerned, they were a loyal set of men, and if they did see the cattle filing past some slumbering puncher, they would go and turn them back, then waken the puncher and tell him to sin no more.

These were things not spoken of before any boss, as no man knew when his turn might come to be caught sleeping at the switch. At times the herd would all be visible from one point; then the boys would bunch up and visit. On these occasions, one could hear stories of adventure that were interesting, especially to young men. One might tell how some fair maiden's heart had been smashed back in the States and was now doubtless mourning for his return, when, if all facts were known, she was flirting with the other fellow.

Day herd was a nightmare to all punchers alike, but no man ever figured out any good way to get around it and still draw his thirty-five per month. Often, while perched on some hilltop, the sun beating down hot enough to fry eggs and no convenient shade, the puncher would dismount and back his horse to the sun, then make himself comfortable sitting against the horse's front legs, enjoying a limited amount of shade. Many times I was sorely tempted to quit the rotten job, yet from some cause I hung on for several years.

At this period of history in Wyoming, during 1885, it was said the range was heavily overstocked, but while there were a lot of cattle, they all looked fat and saucy. At one day's roundup, Mr. Crawford said we had over ten thousand head in the roundup. One could readily believe this statement, should he look down over the roundup from the summit of some hill and see those large bunches of cattle scattered about over an area of country over a mile square. These herds had been gathered from an area of country not over twenty-five miles across in any direction. At this period, this condition prevailed all over the cow country, but after this year the condition would never be seen again.

I crawled into my bed that first night, there to dream of driving herds of bellowing cows and fagged out calves under a blistering hot sun, eating dust by the shovelful and choking for a drink of water. Never in my various experiences have I seen any place I thought was as hot as Wyoming during the middle of the day. However, the evenings and nights were cool, and one could sleep all through the night covered with a blanket.

The second day and all the days afterward were a repetition of the first day; the only changes were climatic. Were the weather rainy, the ground would be slick, which necessitated careful riding while everything was wet. This caused the boys to be more or less cranky.

Once getting a start on this general roundup, our herd grew by leaps and bounds, and after a time our herd became so large it was unwieldy and must be driven to the home range and turned loose. Jim calculated we must have over seven thousand, and they must be returned at once. He planned to have the OS continue along with the roundup, while our outfit must trail the herd home. This would take two days' hard driving.

On throwing the herd off the bed ground early one morning, they were lined out for Lodge Pole, and it would prove to be the hardest drive I ever made. When properly lined out on the trail, the herd stretched out over a mile in length. Of course at this time of year there were thousands of young calves to deal with, some new ones coming while driving along the trail.

When conducting a drive two men acted as pointers, one on either side, whose business it was to hold back the cattle and cause them to spread out and graze or to keep them lined up on the trail. Other men would ride along the flanks of the herd and keep them on the trail while such fellows as myself were relegated to the drags, there to deal with the cows and calves. In this herd there must have been three thousand calves, and each one had a mother from which it had become lost, creating a condition hard to overcome.

Fred and Harry had calculated the distance we'd drive the cattle by noon and so informed the punchers where the next meal could be found as well as a change of horses. To add to the romance of this trip, climatic conditions changed to a drizzling rain, and as a result we had mud, cold and wet weather, and no sleep the first night.

At noon the second day we drove the herd over a small divide, and there, a half-mile distant, we saw the Cheyenne River with its narrow, timbered valley. This proved a most welcome sight, not only to the punchers but to the cattle, which were thirsty, and the leaders broke into a trot. Fortunately our trail led up the river, and there was no effort to hold the herd back. Plunging into the stream the leaders poked up their heads, never offering to take a drink as decent steers should, but heading upstream, walking in the middle of it while the entire herd were at their heels.

After a time the leaders slowed down and drank their fill of water, but the cattle behind continued upstream until they, too, found clear water. During the afternoon we had the herd on Lodge Pole Creek and turned them loose to go wheresoever they wished. The punchers congregated in a bunch, and after a lot of bad language we headed for our ranch, where we would find a red-hot meal and a long night's rest.

On the first day's drive, we punchers would remain in camp just long enough to fill up, catch a fresh horse, then ride back to the herd. This we continued all through this first night, in fact, until we turned the herd loose. Of all the romance tied up in this job, I shall make no mention. Suffice it to say, we lived through it. It brought forth, however, some very unromantic expressions.

As expected, we found Fred and Harry in camp at the ranch, while Fred had his dutch ovens chuck full of food that had a most satisfying influence on our troubled minds.

With the meal out of the way, we took our usual smoke, then rolled up in our blankets, and it was a safe bet that if Fred called us too early there was likely to be a shooting match.

Fred must have had a hunch, for the old boy let us sleep two hours longer than usual next morning, for which we were most thankful. After a fine breakfast we felt much better, so much so that we could talk and laugh at the experience.

There wasn't much to be said in favor of trailing cattle, judging by the experience gained on this drive, and as I thought of those Texas punchers who trailed cattle from the Panhandle country to Wyoming, which required many weeks on a drive, I wondered how they stood the gaff. I knew I wanted none of it in mine, but I was perfectly willing that George should trail the cattle.

At this particular time we had the satisfaction of knowing that if there was another herd to trail home during this roundup, the OS fellows would make the drive. While on this roundup, the idea percolated through my head that if an occasional day was taken off from work, and the men and horses were allowed to rest, more and better work would be accomplished. Yet no such idea had been expressed. It was whoop her up from start to finish.

So busy had we been with the roundup, the glorious old Fourth of July had come and gone, unknown to us. At least, no one spoke of it. Now there was no such thing as a bucking bronc as they were like the punchers—worked to a frazzle—and deserved a rest. The horses differed from the punchers inasmuch as they must spend their off hours grazing grass and getting ready for the next ride.

Cleanliness wasn't given a thought, and as a result we were a soiled, bewhiskered, and mottled-looking bunch. Some were growing thin, and except for my early training in coal mines and blacksmith shops, building up a muscular body and an iron constitution, I might have gone down under the strain. Yet I was able to carry on to the finish, even better than many of the older men.

Two Kinds of Rustlers

IT WAS WHILE HELPING hold the herd on this roundup that a long yearling milled past me which had slipped through last fall without being branded, and now it had shed its mother. Always being a trifle inquisitive, I asked a puncher who would claim the yearling.

I was told it was a "maverick," and no one had a legal claim on it. I had noticed Mr. Crawford had cut these unbranded yearlings into our herd, but what he expected to do with them was still a mystery to me. I learned a trifle later that he would at intervals hold a sale in which all the various foremen would participate. The foreman offering the largest price for them would drive them away and place his company's brand on them, the proceeds going to the Stock Growers Association.

Mavericks were the class of cattle subjected to the rustler's brand, providing the rustler got to them first. Often on this and other roundups I saw mavericks coming in with the herds, so freshly branded that one could smell the burnt hair and flesh; besides, the fresh, clotted blood hung to their ears.

Mavericking, or individual branding of mavericks, was offensive to the Association and caused the Association to spend great sums of money trying to apprehend the rustlers. However, to convict a rustler was practically impossible, even though the Association was positively sure a man was branding mavericks. They found those cowboys were loyal to one another, and even though they knew positively that one of their number was placing a brand on a few head of mavericks, they would never give him away.

Spotters were sent out on the range to work in cow outfits, yet they themselves were soon spotted and made it convenient to get out of the country. Should a cowboy be caught red-handed branding mavericks, or proof obtained of his having done so, he was blacklisted, and no cow outfit in the country would hire him or entertain him at their ranches. Notwithstanding all the Association's laws and rules, some ambitious puncher would take a chance by starting a small herd of his own.

The Association would allow a puncher to own one horse or a herd of horses, yet he dared not own one head of stock, not even a milk cow. If caught violating any of the Association's rules, the puncher was forever damned by having his name placed on the blacklist. In going over this subject in my own way after I was better informed, I thought it an unwise law, as any puncher who had the capability to rustle mavericks was also capable of putting any large outfit out of business altogether and not half try. A lighted match dropped into the dry grass on any range would cause thousands of acres of dry grass to burn, bringing starvation to untold thousands of cattle. Yet the puncher would be strictly within his rights.

To know how the ambitious puncher starts to build up his embryonic herd is interesting, to say the least. The puncher provides himself with a running iron made of three-eighths round iron, with a half circle turned on the end as large as a silver half dollar. The iron is usually fourteen inches long, and after opening a small slit between the sheepskin lining of his saddle and the saddle skirt, it is stored away with but very little danger of discovery. With this iron and a very small sagebrush fire, he heats the half circle and then he can duplicate any brand in the list of brands.

While out on a drive if he should find a maverick and the conditions are right, he chases the maverick down in some draw, then ropes and ties him down, after which he builds his small fire and heats his iron. While waiting for the iron to heat, he will earmark his maverick, then brand and turn him loose—the entire operation requiring only a few minutes if the puncher is expert at roping.

When this formula was made known to me, I couldn't see anything to it but grief for the operator, so I vowed another vow—to leave the rustling to others. This was the operation that proved the thorn to the Association, as they could not, according to law, claim mavericked cattle. Just how a puncher expected to gather his cattle from such a wide scope of country and dispose of them still remains a mystery to me as he would not be permitted to gather his herd on any roundup.

While there were a very few who would try their luck, they were never given away by their fellow punchers, who would thus violate an unwritten law amongst punchers. In a few instances, some puncher either in our outfit or some other outfit would wander into the shop when I was alone and ask me to make him such an iron, to be made so and so, as though I didn't know how. To be sure I would understand, he'd make a diagram in the dust of what he wanted. He usually got what he wanted, and being satisfied he'd offer me a small piece of silver. Then I'd get mad and instruct him to take his contraption and get to h—l out of the shop.

He would leave the shop with a smile on his face and his little iron hid in his shirt, and I knew positively, if the time should come when I needed a real friend, where I could find several of the kind that sticks. One time Jim almost caught me red-handed while I was putting the finishing touches on an iron. As he came in unexpectedly, I saw him first, and one blow of my hammer so changed the shape of that iron I wouldn't have known it myself, thus saving the puncher's hide and my own as well.

I never indulged in this questionable game as I thought my forty per month was plenty good enough for me; yet there were some mighty fine boys carrying little irons, and they knew they had nothing to fear from me.

Looking over the proposition from the puncher's angle, I couldn't find it in my heart to condemn him if he wished to take the chance, inasmuch as the Association had cut off every avenue for advancement for the puncher with one single exception. If some puncher was found to be an especially good cowman, he might possibly, as the years sped by, become a foreman of an outfit; yet the chance was problematical. Only by owning lots of money, or being able to control money, could one hope to be a cattle baron. It was a matter of common knowledge among punchers in those faraway days, that so-called barons could pull off 'most any kind of a deal and get by with it. By their associates, such business was condoned and regarded as big business. However, the puncher knew, and he had a different name for all such transactions.

It was said of one large outfit who found themselves involved in financial difficulties that the general manager found it necessary to make an immediate trip to Scotland and England.[1] For an alibi, he desired to purchase a bunch of fine Hereford bulls, which brought him in contact with the foremost cattle breeders of these countries. While among these men he would extol the many advantages of raising cattle for the beef market in Wyoming. He claimed it cost his company four dollars to deliver a four-year-old beef steer at the railroad ready for shipment.

This shrewd man claimed to be looking for pureblood Hereford bulls so that their herds might be bred into heavier cattle. With more or less of this talk he bought one bull, for which he paid four thousand dollars, and shipped him to Cheyenne. With such talk rampant among these wealthy breeders, they became enthused and commenced fishing for an invitation to visit the golden West and the open range, where they could see at first hand all the things this schemer claimed. To stimulate their sportsmanship, this big rustler told of the cowboys and their bucking broncos. He also spoke of the big game hunting in the mountains and over the prairies.

This line of talk was a potent stimulant, and these wealthy men did everything but ask for an invitation they were going to get. Things couldn't have been more satisfactory to the big rustler, and he returned home with his bull and with the feeling that his company would soon have the necessary kale to meet their obligations.

Hardly had he become settled at home when he received a cablegram that a party of gentlemen were leaving Scotland for the company's ranch. This cable proved stimulating to the manager, and by the time the visitors reached the ranch, the schemer was ready.

In due time the visitors showed up at the main ranch, while the manager was supervising their every activity. After a day's rest, it was deemed expedient to show a few of the many large herds of cattle to the visiting gentlemen. The stage being previously set, the show commenced one morning early in the shape of a large herd of fat steers approaching the ranch. As the herd was driven by, the manager would extol the many fine qualities of the beef cattle that would soon be on the market in Chicago.

The first herd hadn't disappeared before another came in sight, coming from another direction. This parade of cattle continued all through the day, or until the visitors became tired of looking at cattle, and during the evening these gentlemen were shown the Stock Growers Journal with its pages of printed brands, many of which didn't appear on a single head belonging to the company.

After a day's rest the visitors were taken to another ranch, where the parade was resumed, and by evening these men were ready to buy the stock in great blocks. Never for a minute did the schemer tell how many times these gentlemen had looked at the same bunch of cattle as they were repeatedly driven by. However, the punchers driving the cattle knew what a colossal fraud was being perpetrated on these unsuspecting gentlemen. Yet this kind of business was winked at by the man's associates and regarded as big business.

Should this same company desire to buy cattle, each animal must be run through a chute, a tally brand placed on it, and a record made. Parades of cattle did not appeal to this manager when he bought cattle; only when he had something to sell did parades appeal to him.

The punchers claimed to know this was true from personal experience, yet if one of these same boys were caught placing his brand on a little old maverick, he would be run out of the country and his chances for a job destroyed forever.

---

[1] A common practice for securing capital for operating expenses. See Lewis Atherton, *The Cattle Kings* (Bloomington: Indiana University Press, 1962), pp. 189–191.

Making Hay

AFTER A PERIOD of six weeks, the general roundup was over, and we picked up the trail for home and a rest. On reaching Lodge Pole our herd was turned loose; then we rambled along toward the ranch, more dead than alive. Every man had long hair and whiskers and was covered with dirt and grime, yet we were free from cooties.

The horses, poor beasts, were as tired and worn as we punchers, yet unlike the punchers they didn't grumble. However, they were anxious to get at the grass and to be let alone. Quickly we dismounted and turned our mounts into the herd; then Harry took them away where the grass was tall and green and the water pure.

After supper on that evening, we just fell into our beds, exhausted and like dead men. Good old Fred allowed us to sleep plenty late next morning as there wasn't a reason why he should not. For six long weeks we had led the strenuous life, and now we were billed for rest and a lot of sleep.

After a time Fred's nerves got jumpy, and his grub became cold; then he routed us out. After a filling meal we started in to stage the laundry stunt, as there wasn't a clean dud in the outfit. With the washing out of the way, we got busy with razor and scissors, and it was remarkable how the dirty hair and whiskers fell to the ground.

All through the day we dug and scrubbed at the stinking

dirt on our bodies and clothes, and when evening came, we were clean but not rested. After hibernating one full week, the boxing gloves, fiddle and banjo were dug up, as we must have an outlet for our renewed energy. Some indulged in letter writing while a few of us had a decided preference for the gloves.

Not for long though. Jim edged up and invited me to take another walk, which of course led to the shop. "There she is! Fix her up," said Jim, and he pointed to an old rattletrap of a mowing machine.

Of my many accomplishments, fixing mowing machines wasn't one. Yet I never let on but started in on the machine just like I was the man who built them. I greased every bearing I could find on the machine; then I tightened up all the nuts on the thing, after which I ground the sickles. Now I informed Jim she was all set for the small hayfield.

Presently an old pair of white mules were hitched to the machine, and in a short time I heard it clicking out in the field. It seemed most cow outfits had a hayfield where they could cut and stack forty or fifty tons of hay, that the work stock might not perish from the earth during those long winter months. It was my business to keep the machinery part going and the sickles sharp. That we might do this latter job with comfort and ease, Sam and I carried the grindstone out under the friendly shade of a box elder tree, where Sam would turn the stone by the hour while I held the sickle.

During the first afternoon I thought it advisable to make a trip to the field and look over the mowing machine, leaving Sam to take care of the shop. One could imagine my surprise when I found those white mules had turned a slatey color. On close observation, it was evident to me that those poor old mules were being eaten by mosquitoes.

While in the field I heard much rumbling and grumbling about the dadburned mosquitoes amongst the punchers, but despite this small drawback, the haymaking was stepping along. The job of harvesting was half completed, and Samuel and myself were loafing in the shop talking matters over when in rushed Jim and dropped a broken shaft on the floor.

"Can you fix it?" he demanded, and his demeanor seemed a direct challenge; it was plainly evident he was worried and nervous as to the outcome of haymaking. Examining the broken shaft I saw it required no special mechanical ability to make the repairs and started in to do the job. Finding a piece of round iron of the dimension of the shaft, I cut off a piece the exact length, then squared the ends.

"How in the thunder are you going to get those wheels off?" Jim asked, and he was agitated as it looked a formidable job to him. Now it was very well known that Jim was a crack cowman, but I found he didn't know a little bit about blacksmithing.

For reply, I laid both wheels with the broken shaft in them on the fire and warmed up the hubs a trifle. Removing one from the fire I struck it a light tap, and the small pinion wheel dropped off; then the other received like treatment. Yet there were no smiles on his face.

"How in the Sam Hill are you going to get those ditches in the iron?" meaning, of course, the key seats.

"Just watch and don't bother me," I replied and went on with my work. I made a diamond-pointed chisel, then fastened the shaft in the vice, and proceeded to chisel out the key seats. After squaring them up with the file, I keyed on the wheels, and the piece was ready for the machine.

When Jim saw the haymaking would hardly be hindered by the breakdown, he snapped back, and once more the sun was shining as he realized I'd saved somebody a trip to Cheyenne. It occurred to me at this time that perhaps he would trade me a couple of decent horses to ride as all six of my string were down and outers, not fit for anything, and would stumble and fall when walking along a perfectly smooth trail. Yet when the time came that he could have handed me a small favor, the episode of the mowing machine had been forgotten, and I continued to ride the same old crowbaits.

Two stacks of lovely hay piled near the stable were the result of our haymaking efforts, and a great plenty to see us through the winter. Now every man figured we'd get some rest, but, as we learned mighty shortly, Jim had had his head working as usual, and we must get out on the range and brand several thousand calves.

Word was sent to the OS outfit, and a couple of days later we were drilling toward the first roundup ground on Lodge Pole. This roundup was conducted somewhat differently from the general, inasmuch as there was no night guard or day herd though there would be worlds of calves to wrestle the same as on the general. However, because of the lack of men, the country couldn't be covered as quickly. During this roundup, no steer or dry cow would be driven in; they would remain out on the range taking on fat until their turn came later.

Reaching the campground we established camp, and before the job was completed, the OS outfit pulled in and made camp along beside us. Several reps had put in with the outfits, and when a count was had of all the punchers, it was found there were eighty, not half bad for a calf roundup.

We had been in camp less than an hour when a bunch of Sioux Indians pulled in and struck a camp some hundred and fifty yards from our camp. There must have been thirty Indians, counting bucks, squaws, and kids. The Indians had a small bunch of pinto horses, which are a necessity to an Indian. This bunch of Indians was to shatter all my previous dreams of the noble redmen. However, my knowledge had been gained largely from reading yellow-back novels in my kid days and not from actual experience.

With our camp established, the cook found we were low on beef, which caused Jim to send out two men to find and drive in a fat, two-year-old heifer, that class of cattle always being used as beef in cow outfits. I found it was sacrilegious to kill a steer for beef. After a time the boys returned with a good, fat, beef heifer on the end of a rope, and when a few rods from camp, the heifer was shot and butchered, the OS taking two quarters, while our camp got the other two. At the next killing, it would be the OS who'd furnish the beef. With the butchering over, the residue was left on the ground to decompose or serve as food for coyotes or grey wolves. Often the residue of a beef was loaded with strychnine, in the hope it would destroy a few of those calf-killing wolves.

The Indians had been watching this butchering, and the job was hardly completed when here came two bucks pacing into the camp. By means of grunts, signs, contortions, and antics, they tried to make their wants known. They desired to know whether the residue had been poisoned and if they could take it away. Jim knew Indians, and he knew just what they wanted and instructed them to take it away.

Stimulating? Yes, as those two old Indians struck a fast trot for their camp. In a few brief moments here came a flock of squaws with buckets and knives, and by the time they got through with the remains, nothing was left but horns and hoofs. With this operation over, the squaws scuddled for the creek, and after giving those intestines, liver, lungs, and other parts a few swipes in the water, they piled them in their buckets and headed for their camp.

Quickly the Indian campfire was burning briskly, while the pots were boiling, and it was evident the Indians were going to have a feast. When the feast was ready, it was no-ticeable even from camp that the squaws and kids stood back until the bucks had satisfied themselves.

"Say man! It sho am gwan be some powful fine feast," declared Sam. "Want to jine them?"

"Under certain conditions I would, but I'd be powerful hungry if I did," I replied.

Our Relations with Indians

A S TIME WENT ON, I learned a lot about Indians, not the least of which was the fact that they were better sports than their white brethren. I have seen Indians bet the last blanket in their bed and lose, then sleep on the ground and laugh about it. Yet if the puncher lost a bet, he'd whine and beef about the dadburned Indians for a week afterwards.

I found the outstanding characteristic about Indians was that the bucks were born aristocrats and would not work. They required their squaws to do all the work. The bucks will loaf about their camp and gamble if they can find a partner. If they have tobacco, they will smoke, but in the absence of tobacco, they will smoke dried willow bark prepared for the purpose.

A pinto, or a calico horse, is the big joy of an Indian's life, and he will under no condition separate himself from his pinto pony. The Indian differs from the white man in mounting a horse, as he mounts from the right, or wrong side. Usually the Indian rides bareback, and not usually faster than a walk, and for some of their ponies this gait looked entirely too fast.

The government, through their agents, would allow small bands of Indians to go out over the range hunting antelope or deer—anything that would serve them as food. On these trips off the reservation, they might remain away for months gathering their winter's meat. This food took the form of jerked venison or antelope and was prepared by the squaws. As was their custom, the bucks with gun in hand would mount their pinto horses and ride out among the hills in search of food. If a buck were lucky, he would appear in camp with an antelope or a deer on the pony in front of him.

On his dumping it off the pony, the squaws would take charge and would skin and clean the antelope. Afterward they would slice the meat in long strips and hang it on a rope stretched about the camp where it would dry in the hot sun. It would also serve as a fly roost, and by the time it was dry, it had a heavy coat of a protecting matter that was bound to cause sickness of those who ate it. The skin would be tanned by the squaws after the Indian fashion, when it would be called buckskin.

During a summer, many such parties of Indians were encountered and, were it possible, we always paid them a visit in camp, perhaps to strike a trade. Cowpunchers found the Indian blankets were the best saddle blankets one could find, and the boys were always on the lookout for them. To extract them painlessly from the Indians, some game of chance was resorted to, as the Indian loves to gamble. However, the Indians didn't always lose.

It might be a footrace, maybe a horse race, a test of marksmanship, or anything that had the element of chance in it, which always appealed to the Indian. Yet he would lose with a smile; however, if the puncher lost, the Indians would howl with delight.

In my experience with Indians I found they always were in need of four commodities, namely, tobacco, sugar, coffee, and a recommend. With pencil and paper handy, the Indian usually received his recommend but seldom if ever the other three. They prized a recommend above all things and would tote it around and show it to every white man they met, or until the paper was worn out. At times some puncher would incorporate some funny business that would cause other punchers to laugh; then the Indian would get mad, and when he did get mad, he was mad all over.

Even at this early period the Indian had been taught to respect the puncher's six-shooter, for unlike the soldier, the puncher need not wait for orders from the Great White Father in order to shoot a few Indians. Always the Indian would greet the white man by his "How, John!", this being the name of all white men. This was about all the English the older Indians spoke; however, there were many of the younger set who spoke the English language better than we punchers possibly could. This was due to the education the government had given them at some Indian school. Yet when they returned to their people, they laid aside these educational advantages and returned to the wild and nomadic life of the Indian.

This proceeding on the part of the government seemed hardly fair to our thousands of poor children who must go uneducated. Yet they are the ones who must carry forward the affairs of our nation, even though that nation deprived them of their just heritage in favor of an alien people who serve no useful purpose other than to drink rotten whiskey. To me it seemed short-sighted not to clothe, feed, and educate the generation of white children who were to carry the burden of taxation of the future, instead of a class who casts aside the advantages of education and continues to live on the bounty of the government.

On one occasion three of us punchers rode directly into an Indian camp unexpectedly, and here came the Indians and formed a circle about us. There must have been seventy, and all were friendly, while the older ones were begging smoking tobacco. Among the others there was a young squaw who caused one of our number to remark that "she was a peach," he never for a moment suspecting that anyone understood what was said.

That settled it for him, as she lit into him and gave him one of the worst tongue lashings I have ever heard. She did it in white woman fashion, and, what was most humiliating, she used better English than we possibly could. Yes! she was a Carlyle graduate who had cast aside her educational advantages only to return to the wild nomadic life of an Indian.

Our buddy was so embarrassed he rode away and resumed his work while we joined the Indians in having a good laugh. At this period of history in Wyoming, few squaw men still remained. These were men who had taken Indian wives and raised half-breed children. I learned that as a rule these men lost caste both with the Indians and white men; consequently, they lived largely to themselves.

A prolonged yell from Fred at three next morning caused all to bounce out and roll their beds. Even the Indians commenced to move about their camp. Perhaps some old buck remembered there was a small residue still left in the kettles. This morning there were no bucking horses, but all were docile and quiet, as they must have realized there was a hard pull just ahead.

It was orders that while on this roundup no beef cattle must be molested further than was necessary as they must go right along putting on flesh. When this roundup was finished, there should be no unbranded calf on the range. Often, two roundups a day were made from the same camp as the country could not be covered by our limited number of men on one drive.

Usually short drives were made and the branding completed in half a day. At times several hundred calves were caught; then two roundups were impossible. The branding was carried forward with system, enabling us to accomplish much work.

Should the catch be large, four to six men did the roping while many others did the wrestling; then men in sufficient numbers did the branding and earmarking. Wrestling calves was a continuous round of pleasure, romance, and hard work. To understand, one need only to visualize a branding pen a hundred and fifty feet square, half filled with bawling cows and calves, in one corner a large fire with a hundred branding irons heating in it.

The ropers would catch the calf by a hind foot, then drag it close to the fire. One puncher flopped the calf while the other loosened the rope; then both held it down while the hot iron was pressed to its left side, causing the smoke and stink from the burning hair, skin, and flesh to create a horrible condition.

There were other men with sharp pocketknives cutting hunks out of the calf's ears, then doing such other surgical operations as were necessary; then the calf, either a year or a day old, was turned loose and went staggering back to its mother.

Eight to fifteen sets of wrestlers working in the midst of the heat, dust, and bawling caused one to think of an inferno. Yet this was the romantic side of cowboy life and must be endured. Should we have several hundred head to brand, it would require hours of this strenuous work, all for thirty-five per month.

During my first attempts to wrestle calves, the calf had me down as often as I would have it down, a condition that caused me to hesitate and for a moment watch just how experienced men handled the situation. Shortly I was able to bust them as hard as any of the punchers. Our first day's work netted us five hundred calves branded, and believe it or not, we were dog tired and hit the hay with the satisfaction of knowing there would be no night guard.

The only men exempt from riding circle on this roundup were the cook and horse wrangler. Even our various bosses rode like wild men, while horse flesh wasn't taken into consideration. During the weeks spent on this roundup, we worked both our own and the OS ranges thoroughly, and we had branded thousands of calves.

Long ago I found the greatest drawback to this country was the scarcity of good drinking water. Often I have dismounted and taken a drink out of a cow track after a shower and liked it. It was while riding a tributary to Little Thunder Creek that I found a spring gushing out from under an embankment, fully as large as a six-inch stovepipe. This water was clear, cool, and pure. Did we drink? My mount and I filled up to such a degree that we were suffering from pain in our stomachs. Afterward, I have ridden five miles out of my way just to fill up on this splendid water.

At other times one could find nothing but strong alkali water which was fit for neither man nor beast, and even when boiled into coffee, it wasn't fit for man's use. These were the times the punchers were always on the lookout for springs of pure water, which in some sections were abundant.

At the close of this roundup Jim informed us he had had the largest calf crop in the history of the outfit. Yet that old boy said nothing about a horse trade; I continued riding the bummest string of horses in the outfit, and I had a hunch I always would have to as long as I remained working in the outfit.

Presently we returned to the ranch for a short period of rest and a cleanup. Then we must get ready for the beef roundup, which would be a long hard grind, and before we finished, we would have gathered a herd of beef and driven them almost two hundred miles to the railroad for shipment.

Trailing a Beef Herd

ONCE MORE FRED aroused us from a profound slumber and the long, long battle was on. Now the days were a trifle shorter, the horses more worn, and we were unable to accomplish as much work as formerly. Despite this condition, we must fly at them like mad men as a definite amount of work must be accomplished each day and no shirking on the part of anyone.

On this roundup everything was driven to the roundup except the cows with branded calves. We found a few calves that were new since the last roundup, and these were branded. From the first it became evident that no scrub beef would be cut, even though they were rolling in fat. However, their turn would come on the last roundup.

At the start our catch was small, and for a few nights we were able to pen our cattle and avoid night guard. Yet this was only temporary, and presently we were doing our regular shift at night. Of course after the first roundup we had day herd, and to me it seemed there was something about every roundup that took the joy out of the work.

I found the handling of beef cattle a decided departure from handling mixed cattle. Furthermore, it took plenty of grey matter in the head to keep a bunch from stampeding. Should a beef herd make the first run, then it became a constant practice, and before they reached the railroad they would

94

look like a bunch of racers. It was from the profits on the fat cattle that the company received their dividends, so every puncher must be on his mettle while with the herd to prevent this catastrophe.

This work of handling beef proved fascinating, and I enjoyed it as much as any other feature of cowpunching. For this reason I watched closely the movements of the older and experienced men. Furthermore, I wasn't bashful about asking questions relative to the handling of beef herds. It seemed all were agreed it was the punchers' business to prevent the first run, and for this reason they must be alert and watchful at all times while with the herd.

It was a known fact that an old steer would trump up any kind of an excuse to stampede the herd. It might be an old tin can by the trail, maybe a rabbit jumping out from under a sagebrush, or a rattler coiled and ready to strike. Striking a match at night near the herd was dangerous. Easing up on the usual singing might contribute to a run. In fact there were many things that would start them on the run, and after one run, it was run all the time. To check a stampede, it took fast and fearless riders, especially on a dark and stormy night, yet the cowboy did these things and thought nothing about it.

There were steers on the range that the punchers had never been able to land at the railroad. Some were as old as twelve years, and while they were not wild and mean and would suffer themselves to be gathered from the range and placed in the herd, just let the herd be thrown on the trail for a day or two, and it was a different story. They seemed to understand that no self-respecting steer had any business in such company, and they would make a getaway. On the next roundup they would be found in their usual haunts, peacefully grazing and unaware that they had done wrong.

Climatic conditions were ideal all the way round on this roundup, and our work proved a real pleasure. Now the days were growing less hot and a trifle shorter, and while our horses were thin, they seemed to have a lot of staying qualities. Jim had noticed my fondness for the beef herd, and just to hand me a little pleasure, he kept me constantly with them. From some cause unknown to me, I loved to be with those large fat steers, to study their habits and ways to keep them unafraid. Another important factor in connection with this work was that my horses were spared from those hard drives, and it wasn't quite so hard on me.

On the last end of this roundup, a new feature was introduced; at least it was new to me as I watched the boys roast a rib over the hot coals in the evening campfire. After the herd was bedded and the campfire burning briskly, some puncher would slice an entire rib off the quarter of beef, leaving plenty of meat on it; then he'd impale it on a stick of wood after he'd hacked the meat. Now he would hold it over the hot coals and constantly twirl it. When it was roasted, pepper and salt were added; then what a delicious feed one could have.

On the last end of this roundup Mr. J. B. Thomas,[1] the general manager of the outfit, showed up in camp and remained with us until the herd was thrown on the trail. This was Mr. Thomas's first visit to his outfit since I became a fixture in it, and it so happened that on this evening I was the first to start a rib to roasting. Twirling my stick with its precious load on the end over the glowing coals, it commenced to sizzle, and the aroma given off that hunk of meat just naturally created a desire to eat, even though one wasn't hungry. Finally the smell reached Mr. Thomas, and I noticed him sniff a time or two and look toward the campfire.

Knocking ashes from his pipe, here he came on the trot begging for a stand-in on the rib, just like any lazy puncher would do. After placing pepper and salt on my roast, I invited him to cut in, and he did cut in and continued cutting until the bone was as bare as Mother Hubbard's cupboard. With the feast concluded, Mr. Thomas filled his pipe, and after lighting it he leaned back against a cottonwood tree and kept us laughing for the next hour with his wisecracks and funny stories, or until we hit the hay.

In spite of the fact that Mr. Thomas was a Bostonian, he was just a regular guy while with us, sharing our pleasures and hard work alike. Many times when there was plenty of hard work to be done, Mr. Thomas would ride and work as hard as any one of his men, which demonstrated to us that he was no snob, even if he did have an education and heaps of money. While helping us on the roundup, he seemed to know where to cut in so that his work would count most. While working with us, he would never give a man an order but left that to Jim, who had no such scruples. Yet I have seen Mr. Thomas take orders from a raw tenderfoot.

Finally the last roundup had been made, and the beef herd was on the bed ground while Blue and I were doing first relief. Mr. Thomas and Jim were riding slowly about the herd admiring the beautiful beef steers and probably figuring how much kale they would bring on the market at Chicago. Occasionally J. B. would point to some especially fat steer, then pat his stomach and smile. Presently both returned to camp, while we continued trotting around the herd and singing our mournful songs. At the end of our relief we, too, returned to camp, only to find everyone rolled in their blankets sleeping the sleep of harmless punchers.

All were astir early next morning, and by the time the day herders reached the herd, they were spread out and grazing toward Chadron. Presently Mr. Thomas climbed on his buckboard, picked up the lines, and headed south. The last evidence we saw of him was a little whirl of dust away over toward the south, which reminded one of an approaching Kansas cyclone.

Working under Jim's instruction, each man was assigned to a definite position, which he held until the herd was loaded out at Chadron. Two experienced men acted as pointers. It was their business to travel in the right direction and, if desired, to cause the herd to spread out and graze. Other men worked along the flanks of the herd, while such men as myself punched along with the drags. Yet with a herd of this kind, there were no drags.

Jim had all the watering places spotted as we were always able to make water for the noon camp, and if we did make a dry camp on this drive, I do not remember it.

Jim, when not looking for waterholes for the herd, would be spending most of his time with the herd as it was an important feature of the drive. The punchers to the man were on their toes, and each of them felt that he had a share in the responsibility in keeping the herd quiet and unafraid.

Personally, it was a fine experience, and I remember nothing connected with cattle that gave me more pleasure than to jolly along with the beef herd. I had worked with the herd so much I had a speaking acquaintance with every steer in the herd.

We grazed our herd down the Cheyenne River as far as the old disbanded TOT ranch across the river from where Edgemont now stands. That particular spot of ground where the burg now stands was a favorite bed ground with us, and many times I have trotted around a beef herd there, singing our songs to the beef cattle while the coyotes out on some neighboring hill helped on the refrain.

At this time, in 1885, such a thing as a railroad penetrating into our large pasture was an undreamed dream. No one ever spoke of such a thing being possible. Even at that, civilization was making giant strides over about Chadron, and within a few years it would destroy the open range, so far as cattle were concerned.

At this period of Wyoming history, the people in the Territory were supposed to be wild and wooly, yet after spending six years in cow outfits, plus five more in the country, I found a class of men who were real he-men as well as capable men, many of whom could put to shame, so far as accomplishment was concerned, those who write screen plays and libelous books defaming a class of men whose shoe-strings they were not worthy to lace. Such writers would have present generations believe that cowboys were roughnecks, tinhorn gamblers, rounders and shoot-'em-up bad men.

Yet, these same cowboys were gentlemen, and many of them scholars, who had been reared in the best homes and educated in the best of colleges. All were law-abiding citizens who were amenable to existing authority and were splendid gentlemen when compared to the lounge-loafing lizards which infest the best homes and defame the character of real men who braved the frontier with all its dangers in order that a great industry might be carried on to the advantage of the American people.

One need only remember our departed President, Theodore Roosevelt, who punched cows at the time I did. Who would have dared call him a rounder and general bad man? When Teddy called for volunteers for his Rough Riders, who rallied to his standard? I'm sure it was not some cheap fiction writer of cowboy stories who defames the character of departed men.

I have nothing but words of condemnation for those who defame in their writings men who have achieved accomplishment and have been and still are outstanding men of our nation. Among those who might be pointed to with pride by any good citizen are U. S. Senator Joseph Carey[2] of the past; Senator John B. Kendrick, former Governor, now U.S. Senator from Wyoming; and a man I have ridden the roundup with many a day, Harry E. Crain, of Cheyenne, now a leading banker and legislator; and Former Governor Nellie Ross,[3] now a member of the Democratic National Committee. To me, it seems that the pioneer cattlemen are deserving of a more respectable obituary than to be held up to ridicule by a class of men who prove slackers in times of calamity.

After several days spent on the trail we could see smoke from the distant train; then shortly we went into camp for a day as Jim had to go to Chadron and make arrangements for shipping. It was Jim's idea that we should camp a sufficient distance from town so that our herd would not see, smell, or hear those things that attend civilization.

At sunrise the second morning we were shoving our beef herd into the stock pens at Chadron. To facilitate the work, Harry cut off fifty head of saddle horses from his herd and drove them ahead of a hundred head of steers, which would follow the horses into the pens. Once in, the gate was closed, and while the horses were switched into a die pen, the cattle were chased into another.

In this way we were able to pen our herd without mishap or waste of time. However, had climatic conditions been rainy and muddy, the penning would have been a different story. After a time the last steer had been prodded into the stock cars and taken away, and within the hour a long train loaded with our splendid beef cattle would be rolling along toward Chicago while three punchers would keep them company and attend to their needs.

---

[1]Important early-day cattleman and president of the Union Cattle Company, which controlled both the Bridle Bit and the OS Ranches. Thomas was originally from Boston.

[2]Later a U.S. Senator. Carey served as the sole senator representing Wyoming in Congress from 1892-1893, when the state legislature refused to re-elect Francis E. Warren, a former governor, to the Congress. See Osgood, pp. 207-255. E. C. "Teddy Blue" Abbott and Helena Huntington Smith, *We Pointed Them North*, 1939; rpt. (Norman: University of Oklahoma Press, 1939), p. 41, identifies Carey as the owner of the CY Ranch. Carey also served as President of the Wyoming Stock Growers Association in 1884. See T. A. Larson, *History of Wyoming*, 2nd ed., revised (Lincoln: University of Nebraska Press, 1978). See also Robert C. Morris, *Collections of the Wyoming Historical Society* (Cheyenne: The Wyoming Historical Society, 1897), p. 129.

[3]The first woman ever elected governor of one of the United States. Ross was elected governor of Wyoming in 1925. See *Wyoming: A Guide*, p. 7; *History of Wyoming*, pp. 457-460.

Never Again

DURING THE PERIOD of loading, Fred and the night wrangler had moved camp to the edge of town, and by the time we arrived, he had a red-hot meal waiting. With all the good feeling prevailing from the success of landing our herd in the cars, there was much joking and wisecracking among the punchers; even Mr. Thomas took a hand, as he was the most jolly of all. At the time I thought he would have given all the punchers a raise of wages had they asked for it. However, as a reward for all our efforts, Jim declared we'd celebrate two days in town, the celebration to start at once.

As usual, Sam and I hung together while looking over this wild and wooly Chadron, which wasn't wild at all. The town at the time was made up mostly of wooden shacks covered with tar paper while many tents were in evidence. A very few substantial buildings were in evidence, yet they were nothing to brag about.

During this summer the Northwestern Railway had come in from Valentine and continued on west toward what was to be Douglas, Wyoming. Chadron at this time was populated with the riff-raff that always followed boom towns, yet there were many substantial businessmen who saw to it that law and order prevailed. Saloons, gambling places, dance-halls, and kindred places prevailed in numbers, yet there was

101

sufficient legitimate business to take care of the needs of the country. The town was overrun with gamblers and tinhorns or sharks watching their chance to fleece the innocent punchers. Several of our boys did suffer themselves to be gypped out of their summer's wages and went back to the ranch without having bought any winter clothing. Booze caught a few; others bucked the games while some did other things and paid the penalty afterward.

During our stay in town not the crack of a pistol was heard, which was due to a former Texas cowpuncher by the name of James C. Dahlman,[1] who was sheriff of Dawes County and equal to any occasion. Just how Jim Dahlman kept that motley crowd under control was a conundrum. Years and years later this same Jim C. Dahlman became Mayor of Omaha and held the reins of government for many years or until he passed away in recent years, a much beloved and respected man.

While in Chadron on this trip, our fellows held themselves in due bonds, and all were able to keep out of jail until the time came to hit the trail for home. When we did start for home, it was found two men had cut the outfit and remained in town, and afterward I wished I had done likewise.

During this period of celebrating, Jim and Fred had both mess and bed wagons loaded with chuck for the winter's use. Fred went so far as to buy a few bushels of potatoes and a few head of cabbages. In a cow outfit, dairy and fresh vegetable products have no place in a puncher's diet. On cow ranches generally, punchers usually lived on fresh beef, canned tomatoes, beans, and dried fruits, with a little salt pork for seasoning. So it's no wonder we were hungry for fresh vegetables, milk, and butter. However, while the name of cow ranch should indicate worlds of milk and butter, as tens of thousands of cows roamed the hills and prairies, yet milking a cow was never dreamed of.

On this trip home long and fast drives were made, which landed us at the ranch in a few days. Now it was hustle and bustle getting ready for the second and last roundup for the year. The old men knew just what must be faced on this last roundup, and they seemed anxious to get at it and have the agony over. I know I was considerably wiser after I helped on this last roundup.

Our trip to the railroad had given our horses a chance to rest and to fill up, which would prove an important factor on this last job. Now the days were markedly shorter and the nights colder, which caused everyone to dig out their heavy clothes for the occasion.

Pulling in at the starting place we found the OS boys had a rousing fire going, and the cooks soon had the noon meal ready. The hour being early, it was decided to start right in on the job grinding, and we continued the grind until it was over. Jim had announced that the herd would be cut closely as there were too many cattle on the range and many would starve before spring. We tenderfeet quickly learned what Jim meant about cutting closely. Not only were the fat cattle cut as beef, but all old cows and bulls that looked like they couldn't weather the storms were cut into the beef herd.

Lumpjawed and deformed cattle were cut, and everything else but choice stock cattle were driven along with our rapidly accumulating herd; by the time the roundup was finished, we had twelve hundred, many of which weren't fit for glue much less for beef. The punchers were ashamed to be seen with such a herd and called them names.

Without doubt, they were the hardest bunch of cattle ever driven to any shipping point, yet it was orders, and on a cow ranch orders must be obeyed. We found many unbranded calves which were taken care of, and at the finish we realized just what a cleanup meant. Two roundups each day were the order, and in spite of our tired horses and punchers and disagreeable weather, the roundup stepped along.

The OS men like ourselves were working to the limit of endurance while both herds were growing by leaps and bounds. Their herd, like our own, was hard to look at without using profanity. Most of the time while on this roundup, weather conditions were fierce, and if there ever was a thing a bunch of punchers desired, it was to see the end of this roundup.

Wet clothes, rain, mud when the ground was not frozen, damp beds, wet and frozen ropes which must be thawed out before using. We were chilled and cold all the time, especially while on night guard and day herd with no chance to thaw out. Many of the old punchers complained of rheumatism, and if ever a lot of men had an alibi for jumping their job, it was the punchers. Yet every man stuck to his work as no one wanted to be known as a quitter.

We were tired and worn, and it required willpower to keep moving. Had it not been for the shame of the thing we would have quit en masse. Pep? There was none left in man or horse, and we kept going because the boss said go. Despite the glittering generalities indulged in by writers about the lowly cowboy and the romance tied up in cowboy life, this was proving the real thing, and my only regret is that those typewriting romancers couldn't enjoy one experience like this we were enjoying out in the big open spaces with the sky for a roof and the frozen ground for a mattress.

Just as we were on the verge of dissolution for cold, exposure, and loss of sleep and rest, this roundup came to a close. To an inexperienced tenderfoot, the herd looked as bum as we felt and not worth all the suffering we went through in gathering them, yet it was orders, and they must be obeyed in a cow outfit.

With our herd bedded two hundred yards from camp, and climatic conditions threatening, our horses staked near our beds, we started in on what was to prove the roughest night I ever experienced. Even though our campfire was booming and Mr. Thomas and a visiting friend from Boston, a Mr. Ames, an aged man who owned a large interest in the AU7 herd, were in camp, no puncher attempted to roast a rib, as all were tired and sought rest rolled up in their damp, cold blankets.

So tired were the boys that no one suggested stretching the tent, but all of them just rolled out their beds and climbed into them. Mr. Thomas had noted the depression of the men, and for a time he tried to infuse a little life into the bunch, but it wouldn't work as the boys would drop out of the circle about the fire and sneak away to their beds.

"Roll out, Bow!" said a big, husky puncher, giving my tarpaulin a jerk, which caused the snow to tumble into my bed. "Last relief is calling!"

From force of habit I jumped up and commenced to dress, and the language I used was expressive but not to be quoted here. I was shaking with cold as I hustled into my clothes. Finding my night horse, I bridled and mounted him, then rode away into the blackest night I had ever known. No, I did not ride in the direction of the bed ground where we had left the herd as I knew the herd would drift with that storm.

After riding a short time, I let out a war whoop which went unanswered. I continued riding quite a few minutes, then let out another whoop which brought an answering call. Presently I was with such parts of the herd as were left, and by this time other punchers had come up and we took charge. We milled around with the remnants of the herd, and at the break of day we found we had probably a hundred head. The others had gone, and no one seemed to care where. Bunching them up, we drove the remainder near camp and held them, pending relief.

We who were with the cattle saw the cook get up and start his fire; then he cooked his breakfast, after which he routed out the punchers. To watch the discomfort of the punchers as they threw back their tarpaulins and the snow rolled into the beds was amusing, and despite our frozen condition, we had a good hearty laugh.

Finally, all hands ate their breakfast, but no one made any attempt to catch our horses. They stood about the fire and toasted their backs and smoked their pipes in contentment, while we were hungry and shivering with cold due to the fact we had been on duty several hours. Notwithstanding our frozen condition, our temperature soared up amongst the storm clouds.

Harry had his horses bunched by the camp, waiting for those lazy men to get a hump on, yet none did. So sore had we become, we were on the verge of turning loose the cattle when we saw movement in the camp. Presently we were relieved and in camp thawing our frozen bodies, and it was just as well that no one said a thing to us, as the whole ca-boodle looked and acted guilty of breaking a well-established custom of punchers.

We took a lot of time to thaw out; then it required more time to inspect Fred's dutch ovens and satisfy our hunger. With this operation over, we filled our pipes and consumed a lot of time smoking, even though Jim was manifesting symptoms of nervousness as though something were on his mind. Perhaps it was just as well that he kept quiet on this occasion, as he might have started something he couldn't have stopped.

When he saw we had about finished our smoke, he ordered all hands to catch out their strongest circle horses as they had a hard ride on hand. He removed his rope from his saddle, and after thawing it out, he dropped the loop over the neck of a large horse that hadn't been ridden for some time. Leading this horse from the herd, to my surprise he invited me to ride him.

To keep the saddle seats dry, either on or off the horse, the puncher always places his slicker over it and makes it fast to the saddle. In this way he always has dry leather to sit on.

After Jim instructed the punchers how he wanted the country driven, we started out on one hard drive. However, there was no racing of horses this morning as the ground was in no condition for such riding, yet we did strike a moderate speed and kept it up until evening or until we had our herd back on the bed ground.

Now the sun was shining warm, and the snow just faded

away, making the ground slick and dangerous, which in itself would necessitate careful riding. By evening we had our entire herd on the bed ground, with the exception of those outlaws which were expected to get away.

All through the day Old Sol did business, which caused the mud to dry up, and that night stars could not have twinkled brighter. Yes, the campfire was booming, and the ribs, several of them, were roasting, as a general good feeling had been restored and the sore spots forgotten.

It seemed strange how quickly sunshine would restore good fellowship amongst a bunch of depressed punchers, and on this occasion both Jim and Mr. Thomas were dancing around the fire while waiting for those ribs to roast, just like they were kids. On this occasion the boys made Fred's stock of beef look like a dime, yet who cared, as there were plenty of others in the herd.

---

[1]Later sheriff of Dawes County, Nebraska, before being elected mayor of Omaha, serving more than twenty years in that office. In 1882 at the age of 25, Dahlman drove a herd of cattle for the Newman Ranch from Oregon to Montana. For his pay he was given a pearl-handled pistol, a knife, and a holster, which served him in good stead as sheriff of Dawes County. See John K. Rollinson, *Wyoming Cattle Trails* (Caldwell, Idaho: Caxton, 1948), pp. 196-201. See letter from Dahlman to Mullins in Appendix A.

That Kangaroo Court

NEXT MORNING THE SUN was shining and the mud practically dried while the punchers looked and acted happy as the weather man seemed to be working to our advantage after giving us such a raw deal. Our herd was of that type that required no babying, and as a result we trailed right along and in a few days we were penning at the railroad.

With the cattle off our hands and the wagons loaded with chuck, a quick start was made for home as no man knew just when a storm might sweep down out of the northwest and submerge us in snow and sleet. As it was, the nights were fearfully cold, causing the boys to double up their beds and bunk together. Even at that, the cold would come up through our beds and cause us to shiver.

If for no other reason, this condition caused the outfit to get a hump on their movement, which soon landed us at the ranch. The horses, as well as the men, realized we were going to get a long rest, and both alike were anxious to get started at the job. Harry took the horses away, and the poor devils must root, hog, or die from starvation, but no one ever knew of a saddle horse starving.

The wagons were unloaded, then run into the sheds, the camp outfit stored away until another year. Our beds were placed in the bunkroom; then we were ready for our usual cleanup. After this we just ate, rested, and slept for a solid week, and nothing else mattered. Shortly Jim commenced calling the boys into his cabin, the place he called his office, and one by one he handed them their checks for money due. He instructed each to remain on the ranch during the off months, and the first of March their names would be placed on the payroll. Most of these fired men remained at the ranch, while a few packed their beds and visited at other ranches, perhaps to go to work for one of them in the spring. With this job completed, it was found twelve men had been retained under pay, I being one of the lucky number.

After a period of resting, Jim called a mass meeting of all the men on the ranch, and at this time he made the longest speech I ever heard him make at one time. Among other things he said, "We must organize a Kangaroo Court with its judge and sheriff.[1] Rules and laws must be formulated for the government of all who remain on or stay at the AU7 Ranch. These laws when once formulated and posted in the bunkroom are in operation and must be obeyed by all. In the enforcement of the law, no partiality must be shown any individual, and the punishment must be in keeping in conformity with the crime committed. Should anyone, visitors or others, refuse to live up to the law or submit to trial and punishment, he must leave the ranch. This court would be known as the AU7 Kangaroo Court and a court whose laws must be observed by all. Each offender must have a fair and impartial trial while the sheriff is to execute the orders of the court, with power to draft one or every man on the ranch to help, if necessary."

The laws when formulated and approved proved an asset, and it required but one hot trial and the infliction of punishment to convince the men the law meant just what it said. The following are a few of the laws as I remember them forty-seven years later.

"No spitting on the stove or floor."

"No swearing or obscene language in or about the ranch."

"No indecent gestures allowed."

"No toting of guns on or about the ranch."

"No drinking of intoxicants on the ranch property."

"Each man in turn must build fires, carry out the ashes, and empty the spit boxes."

"Each man in turn must chop and carry in wood."

"All must observe all known laws of cleanliness."

"There must be no gambling in any form on ranch property, under penalty of expulsion from the ranch."

Other wholesôme laws were incorporated in the list, all of which preserved, all through the long winter, a clean and wholesome atmosphere about the ranch.

Disregarding the warning by Jim that no partiality would be shown to offenders, his brother Arch committed one of the most flagrant crimes, which called for prompt action on the part of the court, the punchers en masse acting as jurors. The trial went forward with snap to a conclusion, and Arch was sentenced to receive twenty blows with a pair of leather chaps, while he was bent over a chair.

This trial and the infliction of punishment on Arch caused all to take notice that the law meant just what it said, and it never was necessary to call the Court into a real session afterward. Long before spring came, the Kangaroo Court was demonstrated to be a splendid institution, and it was the talk of the cow country. We needed only to call visitors' attention to the law, and in all cases it was strictly observed by them.

To me it seemed Jim's mind never ceased to function, demonstrated by sending those of us who were under pay out to the pine divide to draw in our winter's wood. We worked at this job until we had a pile of wood as large as the ranch building; then he said, "Enough."

After this job was finished, we were thrown on our own resources for entertainment, and it was now the boxing gloves were dug up, while the musical Swede, Colonel Swatky, strung up his banjo, and old Blue tuned his fiddle. These boys were artists, and I enjoyed their music as much as any I have ever heard since, not excepting the radio.

The older men in our group would play cribbage, a game I was never able to learn. At night the beds would be rolled back against the wall, and then we'd put on a stag dance from which we derived much pleasure. Checkers was a popular game, while dominoes were constantly moving. Many indulged in reading some of the very few books to be had on the ranch.

Harry Crain owned a rather large book written a long time before by some man called Bill Shakespeare, and he insisted on having me read the book. To please Harry, I waded into the pesky book and read all about some fellow called Macbeth who kicked up a lot of trouble. I also read about Hamlet and Romeo and Juliet, but it was hard to read, and I filched on the job. Finally I quit the thing as it wasn't my style. I liked books like Nick Carter, Wild Bill, and Jesse James. They were most interesting to me, as some of the characters were still living.

A crazy notion got into the heads of two punchers, which caused them to write a letter to some matrimonial paper called the *Heart and Hand*. They set forth in their letter that they were "two punchers who had picketed on the same rope for years. Now they had grown tired of each other and desired to correspond with some young lady who would be willing to come out to the big, open spaces and share their cabins and wages. A desirable applicant would receive a horse, saddle, and gun so that she might ride out over the prairies and hills enjoying the free wild life of the cowboys. No others need reply."

This letter brought results that were astounding. Never in the wildest flights of imagination did these boys dream of the results that would follow. Two weeks later a tired puncher rode in at the ranch leading a pack horse on which were tied two filled gunny sacks from Hat Creek Store. When they were opened up in the bunkroom, one was found to contain supplies, while the other was filled with mail matter, mostly letters addressed to those two punchers.

Upon dumping the letters out on the table, the boys were invited to help themselves and read every letter in the aggregation of letters if they wished to, but no letter must be destroyed. It looked a formidable task to read all those letters, yet this is what many of the fellows undertook to do. Should a man find a letter which appealed to him, he confiscated the letter and wrote an answer to the writer.

For the next two weeks the AU7 Ranch was the quietest place on the Cheyenne River. All the noise to be heard was the rustle of paper, perhaps a snicker, and occasionally a good hearty laugh. Everyone had the bug. Even Jim spent hours in the bunkroom reading the letters; however, the old boy answered none of them, for reasons I'll explain presently.

Frank Black, a short-legged, dumpy fellow who was born, raised, and educated in Missouri, pounced on the most scholarly written letter in the bunch. After a careful study of the letter, Frank spent several days in composing an answer, and at its completion he requested criticism. The boys were unanimous in pronouncing his answer a masterpiece; then off it went for Arkansas to some fair maiden who had said she desired to correspond with some big western cowboy, and she hoped the correspondence would have a happy ending. Well, it did!

The return letter from Arkansas filled Frank's heart with joy, and from early morning until late at night, he blowed about his sweetie. In due time an exchange of pictures was desired by both, so off went his picture, a recent one made in Cheyenne. After the expiration of plenty of time for an exchange, Frank became nervous and wondered why he had not received her picture. Presently he quieted down and would have nothing to say, and it was evident he was grieving. Hour after hour he would sit in the bunkroom with never a word or smile for anyone, and it had commenced to look like we would have to plant Frank out in some sand dune. Many weeks had passed since he sent his picture, and he seemed on his last legs when a tired horseman rode in from the post office. Dumping the contents of his sack on the table as usual, a package rolled out addressed to Frank, and it was a rare treat to see the smiles return. Now his face was wreathed in smiles, and with a flourish he opened his package while all the punchers crowded around for a glimpse of the individual who had wrecked our little puncher's happiness.

There she was! The largest black mama there was in Arkansas. All had seen the wide grin on her face in the picture, but none could decide whether to laugh at Frank or mourn with him. Consequently, we kept quiet and watched the reaction on Frank. Presently he saw the joke and snapped back into the congenial little puncher we knew him to be.

Naturally, I had my own personal experience with an unknown. However, it had a much different ending, which I shall speak of later. Eventually this letter writing grew threadbare, and we were obliged to resort to former sports for diversion. Well, this business had taken up a lot of idle time and caused many dull hours to pass in a satisfactory way as all those unknowns were not of the type Frank's proved to be.

---

[1]A practice of cowboys on some ranches that constituted the drawing up and enforcing of rules of conduct for that ranch. The men themselves enforced the rules. See Everett Dick, *Vanguards of the Frontier: A Social History of the Northern Plains and Rocky Mountains from the Fur Traders to the Sod Busters*, 1941; rpt. (Lincoln: University of Nebraska Press, 1971), p. 444.

Lost in a Wyoming Blizzard

WITH ALL OUR sports and reading, time dragged, and many of the boys grew restless; yet there wasn't a thing to do about it. Often a desire came over me to be back in what the boys called "God's Country," where I could have a really good time with young folks as nature intended.

Outside the ranch the earth was covered with snow, and fearing the horses would trail away from the ranch, extra punchers would help Harry in rounding them in where they belonged. On one of these days spent out on the range, when the sun caused the snow to sparkle very brightly, many of the boys' eyes became inflamed. The boys were obliged to make hot applications to their eyes and to keep them in darkness. This was the condition of old Hank Moore, one of Harry's helpers, and for a week he made that ranch a veritable hell for the punchers with his grumbling and complaining.

Christmas time came, but all the difference we noticed was a little extra for dinner. Otherwise, the day was the same as all the others. It was shortly after this date that Jim instructed me to go with Arch to the railroad as he was going home to Texas and wouldn't need his horse and saddle down there.

Supplying ourselves with an abundance of wraps and two good saddle horses that had been fed up for the occasion, we lined out on the trail for the 9 9 9 Ranch, some thirty miles

114

distant. Here the boys gave us a fine welcome, and we spent the night with them. During the evening, we ran and re-ran the little wrangler and the Indian. The little racer was particularly friendly to me as he had been told of the deal at the ULA Ranch. We were supplied with a good bed and enjoyed a fine night's sleep. However, the sleep did not prevent the boys from rolling out early as they knew just what was ahead of Arch and me.

From the start we faced a forty-mile stretch across an uncharted country, with not even a cow trail to follow. While on the trip, Arch would repeatedly warn me to watch the landmarks closely, as I would be alone on my return trip. Late that second evening, we reached the Bar T Ranch and enjoyed their hospitality.

The next morning we headed for Oelrichs, eighteen miles distant, and here I was to lose Arch and return to the Bar T. He left me at the railway station, and after packing his outfit on his horse, I led him back to the Bar T and stopped overnight.

On arising next morning, I found there had been a light skift of snow during the night while storm clouds were still chasing each other through the sky. So far, good weather had prevailed, but now it looked like a change was coming. This caused me to want to get over that forty-mile stretch before it hit and penned me up on some ranch.

When I expressed my desire to start, the foreman and punchers set up an awful howl, declaring a blizzard was due and I'd surely get caught. The foreman said it was right-down foolishness to start across that country now, and he wouldn't tackle the job himself; besides, it wasn't necessary, for I could remain with them until spring if necessary.

I was not only foolish, but I was stubborn, so I pitted my judgment against his and lost. The ranch cook offered to provide me with food for the trip, but I declined as I thought I could stand the gaff if the horses could.

Then like the fool I was, I started out on that murderous

trip across that wild waste of country with two horses and a threatening storm for company. The atmosphere was cold and snappy, just about right to make a youngster feel his oats. Everything went lovely until noon; then the storm came down with a bang. Twenty minutes later I couldn't see fifty yards ahead. The snow and ice were pounding me in the face. My landmarks went glimmering, and my only salvation was to keep facing that storm at its worst angle. Should I swerve to the right or left, I would be hopelessly lost, and both my horses and I might perish. Yet I had no fear of freezing, as I had more than enough wraps to protect me. I continued plodding, all the while trying to face the storm in all its fury until late in the afternoon. I found breaks on my right and toward the north. I knew the Cheyenne River was down there somewhere, and if I could make the river, I could have a fire and rest my horses.

Changing my route, I followed those breaks, and shortly after dusk, I came out into the river bottom, which did prove to be the Cheyenne River, which I recognized by the dense growth of cottonwood. Up this river somewhere was the 9 9 9 Ranch, but how far I didn't know. I started up the valley to find out. The storm was raging and the sleet was blinding, yet we plodded along on our lonesome and difficult trail upstream.

At nine o'clock the storm still raged, and then I decided to make camp for the balance of the night. I wanted my horses to have rest even though they couldn't have food. Presently I found a fallen tree behind an embankment, which afforded some protection from the storm, and I dismounted.

Kicking and pulling at the dead bark, I was able to dislodge it from the tree in considerable quantity. Securing a pile of dead wood, I pulled the dry fiber from that bark, and presently I had the flames leaping as high as the tree tops. Removing the saddles from my horses, I covered them as best I could with the saddle blankets, then tied them as closely to the fire as compatible with safety.

With the two saddles and slickers, I made a shelter for myself before the fire, and when it was arranged I was quite comfortable, and had I some hay for the horses and a hunk of Fred's boiled beef and a loaf of bread, I would have been happy even under these trying conditions.

The night was whiled away by smoking and thinking what a boob I really was not to have accepted competent advice from men competent to give it. The thought of prowling wolves or other animals never entered my mind as I had the old Colts hanging to my belt and a large fire for protection.

Before the break of day the storm subsided although the air was biting cold. As light approached from the east, I left camp and wandered out to a hill where I made a visual survey of the country. I decided I was fifteen miles down the river from the 9 9 9 Ranch, and the sooner I struck the trail, the quicker we would have food and warmth.

After replacing the saddles and other junk, we lined out on the trail. I soon found we could make faster time by me walking and leading the horses. This lasted but a short time before I was obliged to pick up a club and drive the horses ahead of me. It was slow going, but like the traditional drop of water, we accomplished the trip by the middle of the afternoon. When we sighted that ranch in the distance, even the horses seemed to realize that it meant food and rest.

The boys at the ranch spotted us in the distance and came to meet us. Mounting me on a fresh horse, they took charge of my tired horses, and we soon found ourselves at the ranch with my feet under the table and my mounts munching their hay in a warm stable. Thirty hours without food under conditions such as we had experienced sharpened one's appetite, and I certainly enjoyed that meal. Only for the fact that the cook warned me that we would have supper after awhile, I might have been eating yet.

Before finishing my smoke in the bunkroom, my eyes grew heavy, and I piled down on a convenient bed and was dead to the world until routed out for supper. This meal proved unsatisfactory as no room was left for further refreshments.

Next morning the sun was shining nice and warm, and my condition was such that I thought if my horses had made a comeback as well as I had, we could reach home. This decision brought forth a howl from the men and the foreman. They insisted that I should stop a few days and rest my mounts, and the foreman informed me that the ranch and the punchers would be on the job even though I remained on the 9 9 9 until spring. If they were gone, he declared, he'd supply me with a string of horses.

I thanked him for his nice offer; however, I was stiff-necked as usual and started home. I had only knocked off half a dozen of those thirty miles, when I found I had made an awful mistake. Arch's horse quit, positively refused to move another inch, and it was evident the horse was through. At first I thought I'd best shoot the old scout and get him out of trouble, but I couldn't go through with it. On the other hand, I unsaddled him and tied his load on my horse and jollied along the trail, leading my horse. We had progressed another half dozen miles when I saw a man approaching. Yes, it was Jim, riding a fine, large, fresh horse, who came trotting up to me. With all the hard luck that had been my lot, there was a brainstorm raging, and my face must have portrayed my thoughts. Jim simply asked about the other horse, then rode off and left me with my thoughts and tired horse.

Plodding along all through the day on this murderous trip, I had a lot of time to think things over relative to my treatment in the AU7 outfit. I asked myself why I must ride the worst horses in the outfit and why I was sent on a murderous trip like I'd made. I had done work in the outfit of a most valuable nature and that no other man could do; besides I'd filled a man's place while on the roundups.

Late that evening I reached the ranch, tired, worn, hungry, and mad. I unsaddled my mount and filled his manger with hay, after which I interviewed Fred, who took considerable pleasure in filling me full of grub. I still remember perfectly after forty-seven years the grief I endured on that trip, and I asked myself many times why Jim did not send an experienced man rather than a raw tenderfoot.

Experiencing a Calamity

SOMETIME AFTER MY return from the railroad, we experienced what was said to be the worst storm within the memory of white men in Wyoming. At a later period it was found that this storm had taken a toll of half of the cattle on the range while small outfits were put out of business altogether.[1]

The blizzard came down on us one evening out of the northwest, striking us with a bang, and in twenty minutes' time we were unable to see the stable. The rain, hail, sleet, and snow bombarded the earth with such force that it seemed as if all living things would be destroyed. We found a trip to the woodpile was hazardous as the sleet blinded one. Some of the boys did freeze their noses when venturing out after wood for the fire.

The cold became so intense that we almost froze in the bunkhouse, notwithstanding we kept our old woodstove red. We buckled on our overshoes, and put on our overcoats and caps even while in the building. Tarpaulins were tacked to the wall to keep snow and sleet from sifting in around the chinks between the logs. It looked like we would freeze should the storm continue long at this low temperature. The Kangaroo Court had to be called in session when some lazy puncher would get the stomachache and wouldn't take his turn getting in wood.

During all this time our principal business on earth was to keep from freezing, and it required action. Fred and his cooking department were put out of business altogether, yet there was no complaint about eats as more important things bothered us. The horses in the stable were seriously neglected, yet none died from starvation or thirst.

The next morning after the storm started there was a solid string of cattle drifting by the ranch, which proved a pitiful sight. The ice and wind were pounding them on their backs, causing them to continue along their death march, hunting shelter, food, and water with none to be found. The water was frozen, the grass covered with snow and ice, while such a thing as shelter for cattle was an unknown thing in the cow country.

Poor old bovines, they would just drift with the storm and bellow until they could go no further; then they'd lie down on the trail and freeze to death. The following spring if a man should ride along any trail, he could count dead cattle by the thousand. This was especially true along the river, where the cattle had sought shelter among the trees and behind steep embankments, evidenced at a later period by finding as many as a hundred who had huddled together and frozen to death.

Wherever one went the following spring, the condition was the same, while the stench from the decomposing cattle was fearful, and one couldn't get away from it. When the spring thaw came, the surface of the water in the river was partially covered with dead cattle floating down the stream.

During the entire summer following this calamity, good drinking water could not be found, unless at some spring, and the wonder was that an epidemic of fever didn't break out among the cowboys. Yet all remained healthy though not happy. Had just one case of fever broken out, there would have been a stampede among the cowpunchers which would have put the cow business out of joint altogether.

The duration of this storm was three days and nights, and

when the sun did break through the clouds, it proved a welcome sight. Then the cattle ceased to drift and commenced to browse on greasewood, which grew abundantly.

To the cattle barons this storm was a calamity, and the country never would come back to what it had been. Win or lose, it was one of those chances cattlemen must take who engaged in the stock business. To a certain extent, with money and nerve, cattle would be restored to the range, but even with both it would be difficult to find men. Should the cattlemen decide to let the remaining cattle restore their former numbers, it would take countless years to come back and perhaps never would be possible.

Some time after this big storm Jim announced that he was making a trip to Texas on a visit, and probably he'd get married before returning. He directed us who were under pay to build him a two room bungalow near the main ranch building. He also directed us to make a nice pole fence about the place, and every pole must be peeled. This must be completed by the time he returned, which would be before spring.

Inasmuch as Arch was already in Texas, Sam Mathers was appointed our boss during his absence, and he would have the power to hire or fire men as he saw fit. Sam vigorously protested against doing anything of the kind, but what Jim wanted, the other fellow had to like, so Sam was boss. "It's shore no place for a woman, no how," Sam bitterly complained to me in private, and I couldn't help concurring in what he said after I had thought of all the inconvenience a woman on the ranch would cause.

Two days after springing this bit of news on us, Jim departed for the sunny south, to be absent several weeks. In the meantime we must build that love nest. Sam's first move was to select from the men two who had learned the art of hewing logs. These old boys could hew a log so smooth that it would look as though it had been planed in the mill. Others were appointed to chop down the trees and trim off the branches while others notched the ends of the logs. My business on this job was to peel poles for the fence. Other men loaded the logs on the wagons and hauled them to the ranch.

When all hands were going, one was reminded of the building of King Solomon's Temple, but while on this job we had a lot of rotten weather. This work proved a blessing to the punchers as it furnished an outlet for pent-up energy. Of course, those boys not drawing pay were not expected to take a hand, yet most of them did as all were interested in that love nest which must be completed by the time the newlyweds returned.

The construction went forward with a snap as the boys had a burning desire to see it finished. As the time came, the frost left the ground, and the building had progressed far enough to start daubing the cracks with mud.

Now I gave Sam to understand I was good at masonry, and as a result I took charge of the only trowel in the country and proceeded to spread that cement, or mud, until the chinks were firmly sealed between the logs so that neither wind, snow, dust, or rain would penetrate through, and it was said that it looked as if a master hand had done the job.

In due time Jim returned to the ranch, but alas, he had no wife. It was shortly after he returned from Texas that Billy Keating, the 4W foreman, drove in at the ranch with a woman. While in Texas, Billy had annexed a wife, and now they were going to stop overnight at the ranch. This was going to be awful, for they would have their meals with us at the long table and those meals—what meals!

As we filed into the mess room, there sat Billy and Mrs. Keating at the head of the table with Jim. Every puncher's jaws snapped together like a steel trap, and they wouldn't open their mouths except for the reception of food. Both Jim and Billy tried hard to induce the boys to talk and be friendly, but there was nothing doing as each man had a fear he'd say something he shouldn't.

During this fearful ordeal, my place at the table was on one side of Mrs. Keating. This caused me considerable nervousness, for I feared she would try to engage me in conversation.

For this spasm of bashfulness we should be pardoned as we had neither seen nor spoken to a woman since leaving Chadron in the fall. Finally Bill broke out, directing this conversation to me by saying Mrs. Keating's name formerly was Mullins. This simple statement on the part of Billy caused Mrs. Keating's eyes to sparkle, and she became very friendly and tried to engage me in conversation about relationships. After considerable display of nervousness, I did confess my name had always been Mullins, and that my father had been born and raised in Kentucky. In their early history one of the tribe had emigrated to Texas, and his descendants were still there for all I knew.

By keeping quiet, we got through the meal without accident, and the same feat was accomplished at breakfast. However, we gave a sigh of relief when the Keatings mounted their buckboard and headed up the river for the 4W Ranch.

---

[1]The collapse of the open range ranching industry across the American West, which came in the wake of several developments. Overstocked ranges filled to capacity by cattlemen in the hope of large profits were unable to support the herds in what proved a generally dry summer of 1885. "The largest roundup in Wyoming" was also matched by such roundups in other areas, and the huge surplus of cattle caused prices to plummet. This development coupled with continued drought and very severe winters in 1885-1886 and 1886-1887 combined to produce exactly what Mullins describes—the end of the open range as it had been known.

On the positive side, the events forced ranchers who continued in the business to examine their operations for cost effectiveness and productivity. This practice caused the adoption of better breeds of cattle, fenced ranges to control breeding stock, and care of stock in winter months to prevent loss of expensive animals. See Walter Prescott Webb, *The Great Plains* (Waltham, Massachusetts: Blaisdell, 1931), pp. 235-240. See also *Vanguards of the Frontier*, pp. 495-496.

Indians Raid the Ranch

Duʀɪɴɢ ᴀ ꜰᴇᴀʀꜰᴜʟ cold spell before Jim went to Texas, a pack of Sioux Indians "raided" the ranch. Having come into the ranch, they made it known by means of grunts, signs, and contortions that they were cold and hungry. In fact, they did look hollow-eyed, cold, and starved. Forthwith Fred consulted Jim about feeding them. At the time, I was helping Fred in the kitchen, and on his return we hustled out an old boiler full of boiled beef which the boys had refused to eat. Also a lot of dried bread, another article of food that was good, but dry and rejected.

All this meat and bread was warmed up, also a large boiler of coffee was boiled, and the delightful odor nearly drove the Indians wild as they waited. They would sniff and jabber to each other while the saliva would trickle down their chins. We found that it took a lot of trouble to keep them quiet until we could prepare the food. Presently we placed the food before them, and it was stimulating to watch how they hogged down that boiled beef and drank the red-hot coffee.

All the while we were urging them to eat, however, they needed no urging as each Indian was intent on getting his fill before the other fellow ate up the food. Soon they commenced to slacken up on the eating as a point of saturation had about been reached. Fred had commenced to think he wasn't going to get rid of all the accumulated beef, so he urged and insisted on them eating more. In fact, he nearly forced them to eat.

They would continue to try to swallow the food, but they reached a place where the food wouldn't go down; then I insisted on their drinking another cup of black coffee. Finally in protest the Indians would draw their hands across their throat and shake their heads vehemently, exclaiming, "Heap full, John." Nevertheless, we urged and insisted on them cleaning up the boiled meat and dried bread until they were as glad to get out of that mess room as they had been to get into it.

The Indians noticed that there was considerable food left, and so they complained, "Squaw, papoose heap hungry." Up to this time we didn't know they had a camp near the ranch with a lot of squaws and kids, so we bundled up the remainder of the food, and they took it to camp. During my years of experience on the range, this was the only raid on a cow ranch I ever heard of.

After a long time, springtime came with its warm sunshine and rains, which caused the earth to take on a coat of green, much to the satisfaction of the horses and what cattle there were left out on the range. Now Jim reminded me of the long trip to Cheyenne for men and supplies, and I must put the wagons in shape and shoe the workhorses for the trip.

Long ago, Arch had returned from Texas and told of the conquest he'd made in the Lone Star state. Of course we common waddies gave him our undivided attention while he recited his adventures, then smiled and kept quiet. Arch was nominated by Jim to act as boss on that long drive to Cheyenne, and when he'd return to the ranch, he would have other stories to tell us.

Personally, I had no stomach for such a trip, as the one a year before was still green in my memory. However, I need not worry about going. When those two men who thought themselves lucky would return to the ranch, they would be broke, with a part of their summer's wages spent in advance long before it was even earned. However, they would have a wealth of information to impart to us stay-at-homes.

We who remained at the ranch were up against a real proposition as our usual forms of sport were worn out, and it was proving a mighty slow life on the ranch with nothing to do but eat and sleep. After a long time, Jim returned to the ranch and reported that he'd hired but fifteen men as the big shakeup in the cattle business had caused all outfits to retrench.

In time the wagons pulled in at the ranch with their loads of supplies while those fifteen tired boys came drilling along behind. Fred gave them his usual treatment, and after they went through the cleaning and sterilizing process, they were ready for a visit and to get acquainted.

I found myself drawn to a young Englishman who had recently come over from the old country to be a blooming cowboy. Just what there was about Fred Penney that caused me to warm up to him, I never did find out. I do know, however, it wasn't Fred's good looks as he looked and acted as though he was out of place on a cow ranch. Yet I found he was a most likable chap even though he seemed green and out of place. Fred seemed to talk a language peculiarly his own, and at times I found it most difficult to understand his gibberish; then he would call me stupid.

If looks could condemn a man, Fred was a goner, and what Jim could see about him that caused Fred to be annexed to the outfit was another thing I couldn't understand. Yet here he was, and here he would remain long after I would have left the outfit. I decided Fred had never done a stroke of work in his life and probably never would if there was any way around it.

I noticed Fred would watch the boys closely when the gloves were in operation, yet no amount of persuasion would induce him to slip them on. As time went on it was evident he wasn't getting the proper amount of exercise, and something must be done about it. Then one day while I was looking for a sparring partner, and having extended Fred an invitation and meeting with the usual result, I decided to start something, and I did all right.

I gave Fred a slight smash on the jaw, and believe it or not, the smash brought quick action. In one-half minute Fred had on those gloves, and he was pounding me all about the place, and the worst of it was, I couldn't stop him. The Indian was easy alongside of Fred, who could punch me any time or place he saw fit, and I couldn't help myself. My arms were entirely too short to reach him, and as a result I took a beautiful trouncing. Instead of getting sore about this friendly but vicious bout, it cemented a friendship that had been going on some time; furthermore, it caused me and others to enlarge our respect for Fred.

When it came to work, Fred was zero. To do his best, Jim couldn't get much out of him, and how the boy held his job was a mystery. When the roundup started, Jim did find a place for him that exactly filled the bill, and Fred declared he liked to wrangle the blooming horses at night.

When we went out to fix up branding pens, we saw firsthand the results of the big storm. Wherever one turned, there were dead and decomposing cattle while the stench was fearful and could not be escaped. The streams of water and the water holes were a mess, and how we would be able to go through the summer's work without an epidemic was a conundrum, yet we did go through.

This experience didn't elevate our spirits, but all were low on pep to go ahead. Some spoke of leaving the country, and a few really did, yet most of the men hung on. We realized that never again would we see the large herds of cattle; neither would there be the same feeling existing as there had been the year before.

Many spoke of the condition as being the end of the cow game, but to me the danger was slowly and insidiously approaching from a different angle. That Northwestern Railway continued building west from Chadron, and during the summer it would reach a point that would be Douglas, on the Platte River. This railroad would bring hoards of settlers, who would settle along the best streams and enclose the water away from range cattle, which would more surely eliminate the cattle than all the big storms.

Money and nerve would restore plenty of cattle to the range, but both combined could not restore the water to range the cattle. To be sure these settlers would have small bunches of cattle, perhaps similar to our town herd, yet it would be starvation business and would cause a condition in Wyoming from which it would never recover.

The first of June the horses were run in the corral and the parceling gone through. At its conclusion, I found I had drawn the same old string of benches which no other man would ride. This caused a minor brainstorm, yet I bided my time and accepted them as though I'd been handed a favor. I seriously thought I would hunt a job in some other outfit, but I realized I had been kept under pay through the winter and was drawing better wages than any common puncher, so I decided to stick around for a while longer.

Of course, the town herd had been worked; had they not, they would have piked back to the range with their feelings hurt and might not come back again next fall. Naturally the new men enjoyed the show, but to my way of thinking the heart had been taken out of the sport due to the big shakeup in the cattle industry.

Depression Everywhere

IN DUE TIME our two outfits trailed away toward the general roundup ground of last year. We were billed to work the same territory as last year, and while riding along the trail and watching the new tenderfeet, I wondered how it came about that they rode better horses than I, whose services were most valuable to the outfit as a blacksmith; besides, my efforts on the roundup were just as valuable as any other puncher's.

As we trailed along, the punchers tried to be jolly, yet it was only a veneer to cover the real feeling in each man's mind. After a trial at this the boys lapsed into silence, each man busy with his own thoughts, and had a stranger met us, he might have thought we were attending our own funeral.

The day or so spent in camp before starting the work was spent in moping about. Now, there were no fast or slow races, as all outfits were afflicted the same, and if there was a thing they desired, it was to be let alone. The morning set for work we rode out to the meeting place on the same hill, where another gloom was evident.

In numbers of men, the outfits had cut down a third from last year, and there was scarcely a smile on any man's face. Perhaps it was my imagination, yet I thought the horses had caught the disease as not a bucking horse was seen—a very unusual thing at this time of year. Of course Jim was roundup foreman, and forthwith sent out the drives as usual, but the cattle were not to be found, and our work was soon finished. We headed for the scene of the next day's work, but our catch was small and it was evident the storm had taken its toll. On this roundup, it wasn't found necessary to throw back cattle, but our herd was held all the way round.

When we returned to the ranch from this roundup, no one was tired. Even the horses were fat, and it seemed as though we had been out on a scouting party rather than a general roundup. Rest and sleep not being necessary, Jim sent the boys to the hay field, and in due time the haymaking was finished. Now we were subjected to enforced idleness, a thing none desired. Our usual sports were passed up, and the boys would sit around and meditate, talking in low voices of the calamity that had hit the cow country with such telling effect.

After ages we went out on the calf roundup, but the calves were not there, and as we were not interested in other kinds of cattle, our work was quickly completed. At the conclusion of this roundup it was found that the calf crop had been cut in the middle. The short calf crop was another cause for gloom as experienced men knew it would require years to build up the herd from the increase. Of course, cattle could be shipped in and the range restocked, but it was evident the owners had sidestepped investments of this kind at this time. As had been predicted, settlers were squatting on the best streams, fencing the water and bottom land away from range cattle. Another destructive force had been reported coming into the country in the way of large bands of sheep, which were poison to cattle. It was said much of the best range land was covered with them. I was told that the sheep ate the very roots off the grass, which destroyed the land for both cattle and sheep. It was found that to a large degree the sheep did destroy the range, and they proved a potent factor in eliminating the cattle.

After the calf roundup we returned to the ranch, billed for another long period of loafing. Jim had told us that there would be but one roundup; however, it would be a cleanup. Nothing would be left on the range but choice stock cattle and young beef steers. This information led the boys to believe another couple of years would see the end of the old AU7 outfit; however, it hung on for several years.

We had been at the ranch but a week when a strange cowboy put in with us. He claimed to have come from a new town over on the Platte River, which would be known as Douglas and perhaps would be the terminal of the Northwestern Railroad. This young man was especially confident that Douglas would speedily become the state's capitol due to its central location and its being a distributing center.

He painted such a glowing picture of Douglas and its possibilities that I became interested and asked many questions as to the advisability of starting a shop there. I was sure this distributing center would head off all those long trips to Cheyenne with freight teams, and it would be best if I could get in on the ground floor.

Counting my finances, I decided I had sufficient to start nicely, and if I were lucky in getting business, I would have an independence I'd never known. Furthermore, I could grow with the town, and my future would be just what I made it. At this time I was in my twenty-third year, and it was time I should be doing things on my own hook. Yes, I would, sink or swim, give the proposition a trial.

Should I fail! Oh, well, I was young and full of ginger and could try again. On the other hand I was firmly convinced the cattle business was headed for the rocks, and before long the end would come. Dwell on the cow game as much as I would, I could see no permanent future for the cows or the open range, and the time was ripe for a venture on my own hook.

Hunting up Jim, I laid the entire matter before him, and while he said nothing to discourage me, he said nothing to encourage me. However, he did ask me to clean up what accumulated work there was about the shop; then he would provide me with horses for my trip to Douglas.

At once I slammed into the work, and after two days everything was shipshape and I was ready for settlement, the first time since I landed in the outfit. With this small matter out of the way, I had a check in my inside pocket for three hundred and fifty dollars, the largest sum of money I ever had at one time up to then.

Jim instructed me to write to him if I went on the rocks. It was quite a satisfaction to know there would be a job for me if I should need it and desired to go back to the range. At last my bed was tied onto a pack horse, and after telling the fellows, "So long," I mounted my saddle horse and headed out on the trail, hunting the magic city of Douglas. Landing in Douglas the second afternoon, I found a temporary town made up of tents and tarpaper shacks and a population estimated to be one thousand people. The citizens, like those of all western boom towns, were made up of the riff-raff, or floaters, who always followed boom towns.

Yet there were many prosperous-looking businessmen looking for a location to enter business. A quarter mile south, the new town site was staked out on a sagebrush flat, and it was a most ideal location for a town. Securing a plot of the new town, I selected a location for my shop, and when the sale started a day or so later, I bought my lot.

Two hours after the sale started I had bought my location and had carpenters sawing and pounding on my new place of business, and had it not been for an ambitious Chinaman, I would have had the first completed building in Douglas in the year 1886. With my shop completed, a new set of blacksmith tools were installed, and by the time I was ready for it, business commenced to come in.

Business continued good until late in the fall, when the freighters holed up for the winter, and my source of income ceased. Now it was evident; I must look elsewhere than in my shop for a living.

Since that time I have heard people speak of Douglas and what a wild town it must have been at the start. They seemed to think that a man must go heavily armed and would take a long chance on his life every time he stepped out on the streets. Yet after spending several months in Douglas at the start, I had never seen or heard the bark of a pistol. During the entire time I spent there I never saw any trouble that the authorities couldn't take care of. To be sure there were saloons, gambling houses, and dance halls, and they were largely patronized, yet it was done in an orderly way. The inhabitants seemed law-abiding citizens and neither gave any trouble or made any disturbance.

The aforesaid businessmen had taken care of this feature by placing men in office who could maintain order and safety. Should some tough character blow into town, the officers were the first to be advised, and they would instruct the undesirable to behave himself or move on.

During my time spent in Douglas it was my fortune to see one of the foremost and most notorious characters of the Old West. Calamity Jane was soundly sleeping one hot afternoon, curled up on the music platform in a dance hall. Her slumbers were of the stertorous or jerky order, and occasionally she'd give a snort which caused me to believe that the end for Calamity was at hand. Yet she survived the ordeal and lived to a ripe old age.

During Calamity's slumbers, flies by the hundreds swarmed about and into her mouth and nose, yet the attack went unnoticed by Calamity, and she slumbered on and on until she got through slumbering, or, in other words, until she sobered up.

The picture of Calamity presented to my youthful mind at the time still remains, though I fain would forget it.

Driving through Douglas in 1932, I saw it had grown into a charming little city, with well-kept homes, churches, and business buildings. Splendid school buildings were in evidence and a credit to the municipality.

Being unable to make a living in Douglas, I hustled for a job, which I found twenty miles east of Douglas at a new coal mine being opened up at a place they had named Shawnee. Having landed a good job and a boarding house, I made good as a coal miner, a line of work I had learned in my very youthful days. During the balance of the winter I had a nice time and was able to save a few dollars on my next stake.

In February I received a letter from Jim, offering me a raise of five a month if I would return for the summer. Well, I knew coal mines, and I knew with the coming of summer work would slow down and one would hardly be able to eke out a living. It was this knowledge that caused me to give Jim's letter serious consideration.

I also remembered the rotten string of horses I'd ridden two years and would doubtless ride again if I returned. I thought of the punchers, the horses, the cows, and how lonesome they'd be if I wasn't sticking around. I thought of old Fred and the puddings he'd make occasionally; then there was Harry, sputtering around with his horses. The call was too strong for me, and I couldn't resist it. I was willing to endure all the drudgery and hardships that might be with the punchers, some of whom I liked very much.

Not yet had this cowpunching got out of my system. It had a hold on me like the hold of a narcotic on its victim; the more one got of it, the more he wanted. I knew I was willing to face the hard problems of cowboy life just for another dose.

Breaking Broncos

THE GOODBYES WERE said to my Shawnee friends, and I mounted a train and headed for Lusk. After I spent an hour on the train, it whistled into Lusk, where I dismounted. As I expected, a puncher stood waiting for me at the station, and we proceeded to pack my bed and outfit; then, saddling a spare horse, we lined out for Hat Creek Store. Here we remained overnight with Mr. Storey, who had many questions to ask relative to Douglas. Being rather loyal to Douglas, despite the fact I went broke there, I painted rather a nice picture of the coming state capitol.

In due time we reached the ranch and disposed of our horses; then, after locating my bed in the bunkroom, I once more became an AU7 puncher. It sure was a glorious feeling to be back with the punchers and to participate in their activities. Fred, the cook, seemed too attentive, yet it was only his expression of welcome. Jim and the punchers seemed glad to see me, and it was now I had visions of a good string of horses; perhaps I would be invited to carve, maybe to represent on the outside.

It was after the evening meal while visiting in the bunkroom that a puncher spilled the beans. Now I learned for the first time that the outfit had bought forty head of Oregon broncs, which ran in weight from eight to twelve hundred pounds and were from four to nine years old and not even

136

halter broke. I was told these horses would be parceled out to the experienced punchers, two for each man, and they must break them to ride.

This news came as a shock, as I had learned outfits who broke in green broncos always hired a bronc buster for the purpose. This was due to the big storm which had played such a disastrous part in depleting the range cattle, and all the outfits had tightened up on expenses. This was an unwelcome departure from the old way and caused a lot of grumbling among the punchers. Yet, there wasn't a thing to do about it.

The company, or rather Mr. Crawford, did retain Billy West, the man who drove the broncs through from Oregon, to take care of any bad horses the punchers couldn't ride, and it was perfectly wonderful how Billy could subdue them and make the horses like it. However, Billy wouldn't ride bad horses as a steady vocation.

Evidently we were up against a real proposition. As long as the horses had to be broke, I would undertake to do my part, but I wouldn't tolerate any interference in my method from anybody. During my short turbulent life, I had had a lot of experiences with wild horses and mules in blacksmith shops, and I knew from personal experience that shoeing mean horses was a lot more dangerous than riding them, and this would be only another experience.

As time went on, I heard a lot of rumbling and grumbling about broncs. It was bronc for breakfast, dinner, and supper, then on until time to hit the hay. Several boys thought they would chuck up their jobs, but none did as they might find a worse condition in another outfit.

Jim had no hesitation in telling me to clean up what blacksmith work there was as more important things must be attended to. Yet this important work did not worry me as it did most of the other punchers as I knew just what I was going to do. The punchers spent all their time discussing broncs. It was bronc all the time until we found ourselves lined up on the corral fence with our hackamores in our hands, like a lot of condemned criminals waiting for execution.

Anyway, it was going to be a great adventure, but in a way I didn't mind it so much as I had decided to go through the ordeal in my own way, and if anyone butted in, they could ride the broncs themselves.

With those wild horses in the corral and us punchers lined up on the fence, Jim, Arch, and Sam entered the corral with ropes in hand; then the Wild West was on, and what the boys were to witness would throw a chill in most of them. Personally, I thought it great sport to watch a rope settle down on some bronc's neck and watch him fight back.

He'd pull back, plunge forward, strike with his front feet, and kick out with his hind ones as he choked on the end of the rope. With the bronc almost choked to death, Jim would call some puncher by name and tell him to come get his bronc, name, and ride him. The first puncher to draw a horse turned white, then red, and back to white, as he slid off the fence. His knees were knocking and his step halting as he approached that ferocious wild horse, and with the help of Sam or Arch, perhaps both, they would fight the bronc until they had the hackamore on him.

Just to sit on the fence and watch some wild bronc fight was a sight that would throw a chill into any man's anatomy if he knew he was going to be obliged to ride him or chuck up his job. No, this stuff didn't look so good to any of us; but it was break bones or get out of the outfit.

Jim's rope fell over the neck of a large, squatty, bay horse which must have weighed twelve hundred pounds and was wilder than a black-tailed deer; then he called for me. The job looked bad for me, and I knew it would be some undertaking to subdue that wild beast.

I knew the job was no more dangerous than to shoe a bronc's delicate hind feet, but I must approach my job from a different angle. I always figured horses were amenable to kind treatment, and I was going to try it out on my two broncs, even though it was a decided departure from the old way of breaking horses.

After a hard struggle, I had my bronc out of the corral and christened him Shawnee, after the mining camp I worked in the previous winter. My first efforts were directed toward teaching him to lead and to get on friendly terms. This required hours of tugging, pulling, and petting. After a long time he lost his fear of me; then the battle was half won. Presently he would trot along behind me, and he seemed to enjoy doing so.

From force of habit, I commenced monkeying with his front feet; then I passed to his hind ones until there came a time when he submitted to me raising one from the ground. I will state at this point that "if a man would successfully break horses, he must show no fear of them."

The punchers who watched my method declared I was nutty; yet I thought I had a clear conception of what I was trying to do. Within two days I was riding Shawnee bareback, and a hackamore on his head. Then I was accused of being crazy; even Jim gave me a few caustic looks, yet he let me alone.

Soon, now, I familiarized Shawnee with the saddle blankets; then presently I had the saddle cinched on him, rather loosely at first. Then within a day I was riding the old scout everywhere, with never an offer to buck or otherwise misbehave. Kindness and perseverance, perhaps a few lumps of sugar purloined from Fred's mess-box, did the business.

Shawnee and I became regular pals. When I'd throw my rope over his neck, he would suffer me to lead him from the herd and quietly saddle him. It seemed my way of breaking broncos eliminated that holy fear they had of cowboys, and when this was accomplished, it only remained to teach them how to be useful.

The old way of breaking horses to ride would for a long time create a circus every time the horse was ridden. To illustrate, each time a horse was dragged from the corral and the hackamore put on his head, he was snubbed to a saddle horn, and he'd be led around by the hour or, as I thought, dragged around in order to teach him to lead. With this accomplished, it was a battle royal to get the saddle cinched on him, and with the puncher in the saddle, the bronc would be led around other hours with his head so tightly snubbed to the saddle horn on a gentle horse that the bronc could neither get his head up or down, consequently no bucking. However, when that bronc was cut loose from the leader, it was a different story, and some puncher was apt to hit the ground if he wasn't a crack rider. Naturally, each time the bronc was roped from the herd, he understood that he must go through with all this Wild West, and believe me, in many cases it *was* Wild West.

When any bronc got so nasty that the puncher couldn't ride him, Billy West was the boy to trim him down. Billy remained with the outfit until the last buck had been left in any bronc; then he scooted for the big open spaces out in Oregon.

This riding school went forward with a snap. Many punchers had hit the ground, yet the broncs were settling down and becoming very good horses, though a few jumped high and hit the ground hard. Presently we got to riding away from the ranch under the supervision of men on gentle horses, who would haze some runaway bronc from a ditch or other dangerous place. Perhaps it would be after some bronc who had thrown his rider. These rides greatly enlarged the broncs' experience, and they were taught to serve man in a useful way in return for the Wyoming bunch grass they ate.

We rode three weeks; then the riding came to an abrupt end, and we must go out and fix branding pens. The broncs were taken away by some older punchers, who would ride each in turn. Up to now neither of my broncs had bucked or otherwise misbehaved, and I inwardly congratulated myself. My theory had proved a knockout, yet I had endured many rotten suggestions from the boys.

Badly Punctured

HAVING RETURNED FROM the range, the entire horse herd was run in the corral at the ranch and the parceling gone through with. At the conclusion, I had been handed four of my old string and of course my two broncs. This caused a feeling of resentment, but what could a fellow do about it?

Without waste of time the riding school was taken up, and of course my rope circled old Shawnee's neck. I led him from the herd and placed my saddle on him. I noticed the horse gave me a peculiar look, yet he stood quietly and allowed me to mount him; then things commenced to happen.

Shawnee leaped so high I had a hunch we'd never light, yet he did come down and hit the earth like dynamite and have a cough that was frightful. I received a jolt that jammed every bone in my body; besides it caused me to lose both stirrups and to grab the saddle horn. Going up the second time his back was curved like a rainbow, his head tucked between his front legs, and to add to my misery, he whirled halfway round. Returning from that trip I was still clinging to the saddle horn, yet dangerously to one side, and to me it looked very much as if something was going to happen mighty quick, and I was going to lose my reputation. I did all right the next jump, when I found myself sitting on the ground with Shawnee standing there looking at me.

Shaking myself to see if all parts had come down together

and that there were no broken bones, I walked up to Shawnee, and he suffered me to take hold of the reins and mount. Never had it occurred to me that old Shawnee, my favorite horse, would hand me a package like this, and I decided I would watch him a bit. Taking my quirt from my saddle horn I hung it on my wrist, as I felt reasonably sure he would do it again.

Presently we were trotting across a flat prairie near the ranch, while the boys were discussing my flop, when a puncher came loping up from behind. Apparently Shawnee was scared, and he commenced to do it all over. However, he found it slightly different this time, as I socked those sharp spurs deep into his side and held them there. At each jump, they'd scrape his side, causing the blood to flow freely. At the same time I was working my quirt over his head, or as much of it as I could reach.

This punishment came as a surprise to Shawnee, and it caused him to do some fast work; yet I hung onto him and continued my punishment. The old boy found it a very different job this time, as those sharp rowels were cutting great gashes in his sides at each jump, while the blood was trickling down his belly and onto his legs. Both of us were sweating, yet the show went merrily along, while the punchers were howling words of encouragement which I didn't hear.

The punchers had formed a circle around us, watching the exhibition, all of them expecting to see me hit the ground. As much as the horse twisted, jumped, and whirled, I held my position in the saddle and continued to punish him. This time I decided to have it out with him once and for all, and he would have learned his lesson when he got through. Shawnee must have decided it was no use, and he commenced to slow down, yet I continued roweling him even harder. Now the boys ceased to yell and stood waiting for the outcome, and, were the truth known, their sympathies were with the horse.

It was my party, and I didn't care a rap what anyone

thought. I was the fellow who was breaking this horse, and if I could do it, it would be done well. Soon Shawnee wanted to quit, but stubbornly I continued the punishment. Presently he ceased to buck and would stand and kick at my spurs. Soon he quit kicking and would only flinch when I spurred him. I decided the punishment had gone far enough and dismounted. Dropping the reins over his head, I walked around in front of the horse, and he made no attempt to run away.

This battle broke Shawnee of bucking, and he was a well-behaved horse as long as I rode him. Afterwards I was told that the two Texas punchers helping care for the horses at the horse ranch purposely made Shawnee buck, which was a scurvy trick, to my way of thinking, inasmuch as they hadn't a thing against me except that I drew ten a month more than they. Anyway, the incident passed. My horse was thoroughly broken, I gained some reputation as a rider, and the experience added to my overplus of conceit.

This riding school came to an end, and our preparations were made for the general roundup. The horses were allowed to fill up for a short time longer. Well, I was betting Shawnee's sides were sore, but it remained with him whether his wounds would be opened up again at the next riding. I found, however, that he was sensible and behaved nicely.

George, my other bronc, was selected for the morning's ride when we started for the general roundup. George was developing into a single-footer, a most desirable quality in any road horse. George had proved a self-respecting horse, never indulging in that low brow stuff called bucking. I had the most profound respect for George and his admirable qualities. On this morning George was a dignified horse as we trailed along, mindful of what the other broncs were doing.

After we had traveled two hours along the trail, we started descending a long, sloping hill covered with sagebrush and numerous beds of cactus, seemingly happy. However, from some unknown cause George leaped into the air and commenced to squirm and buck, and he twisted so fast it kept me busy staying on him. Yet I was doing a respectable job of riding until my right spur pulled over my heel, and whang! I landed in the midst of a large bed of cactus. George must have leaped over me, and he either kicked or struck my right arm, which caused me to believe it was broken. Any man who knows the Wyoming range will instantly recognize what a jam I was in. The boys rushed up to the margin of the cactus bed and halted. Just how to fish me out was a problem, yet after considerable time the feat was accomplished; then an examination of my arm was made. While the flesh was bruised, no broken bones were found, which was, in a measure, a relief not only to me but to Jim, as it was a hundred miles to a doctor. To me, my sore arm was only a side issue compared to those cactus thorns which had penetrated my anatomy from all angles, a thousand times worse than porcupine quills. George was caught and unsaddled, while Harry rounded up his horses, and a gentle horse was caught out for my use. With the help of the punchers I was placed in the saddle, but when I undertook to sit down in the saddle— well, it couldn't be done. I just didn't sit but rode to the noon camp standing in my stirrups.

Upon reaching the noon camp, trouble commenced for me, and it would be many days before it ended. Reader, visualize if you can big thorns, long thorns, short thorns, crooked thorns, straight thorns, and all other kinds of thorns plunged into your pelt up to the breaking-off point, then broken off even with the skin. Could you do this, you would realize the unfortunate needs a friend.

With efficient help I dismounted, and after my bed was rolled out, I removed most of my clothing and lay down on it; then business commenced. With a pair of sharp-pointed pinchers carried by the cook for the purpose, a lusty puncher started an operation that didn't end for weeks. The operator would make a dive down in the skin for a thorn; oh, well, it was what General Sherman called war. Hour after hour the boys would work in relays, prying and digging thorns.

Some lusty puncher watching the operation would become interested, open his pocket knife, and start operation. After several days of effort and torture, the last outlaw thorn was captured, and I found myself in much the same condition as Shawnee did, completely whipped. Never afterward was I able to give a cactus a friendly look, much less a kindly word or smile. In fact, I never did determine what useful purpose cactus served; yet they were more than numerous all over Wyoming.

I was told that large cactus beds served as admirable protection to young calves, antelope, or deer when grey wolves got after them. It seemed these hard-hoofed animals would make a run for a cactus bed and leap into the middle of it, while the wolves would halt at the margin and circle around the bed, never daring to venture in. They would circle about it until they grew tired, then leave in disgust.

The general roundup started on schedule, but my sore arm and other parts prevented me from taking an active part in the work for several days. Yet leave it to Jim to see to it that I made a quick comeback. He prescribed day herd; however, his treatment had only negative results, much to his chagrin. It failed utterly to reduce the swelling of my arm or to cause the several hundred other wounds to promptly heal.

The boys rode my broncs in turn, and by the time I was ready for them there wasn't a buck left in either. Twice I had been squarely dumped since landing in the outfit but not conquered although Jim gave me a horse later in the summer who had me bluffed. This roundup fairly flew over the country, as there weren't cattle enough left to amuse us, much less cause us to work. George was neither forgotten or forgiven, and I couldn't understand why he had handed me such a scurvy trick. I tried to figure out an alibi for George, but go over the situation as much as I would, I couldn't find one reason for his action, so I decided to make him pay.

If possible, George was ridden on every hard drive; then I'd ride him between times, that I might in a measure settle with him for that dose of thorns and the prolonged surgical operation. Many times over he paid the price, yet the temptation remained to send him to the limit, especially when I thought of cactus thorns. By the time I was through after the beef roundup, George was only a shadow, and very quiet and docile.

The prescribed country having been worked, we pulled in at the ranch, where a short period of resting, or rather loafing, was endured. However, it wasn't for long, as Jim declared we'd make the calf roundup. Climatic conditions were ideal for this roundup, and to our surprise we branded a large flock of calves, so many in fact, that it caused Jim to smile, a thing he'd hardly done since the big storm. At the end of this roundup we found our broncs were rapidly learning the cow game, and no puncher had been killed or badly maimed.

A Tough Deal

A FTER A PERIOD of loafing on the ranch, we headed out on the beef roundup, which would be my last roundup in this outfit. Jim passed out the word that the herd would be cut close and all cattle must be driven into the roundup, and after we started cutting, it looked like the AU7 outfit was going out of business sure enough.

When all were bunched for the first drive, it proved a fairly representative bunch that lined out on the drive, and believe me, we led a fast life that morning. I was riding Shawnee among the leaders, as I had no fear of being set on foot when riding him.

Everything, even antelope, were driven in during this roundup, yet those pesky antelope would make a getaway before we'd round up the bunch on the ground. The herds were worked as usual, calves branded, and even a few mavericks showed up in the roundup, freshly branded. This caused Jim to frown something fierce, while the punchers would slyly smile and wink at each other.

This beef roundup surely stepped along, and even before we realized what it was all about, we were heading out on the last drive, which was to be a long, hard one up Mule Creek near the 9 9 9 Ranch. On this morning I had selected to ride that horse I was a trifle afraid of as I wanted to hand him a package. However, I quickly found Jim had other ideas

147

about my activities on this particular morning. When we were congregated for the drive, Jim ordered me to Lusk to send the old man, Mr. J. B. Thomas, a wire stating the date of shipment.

Not caring to make a trip of this nature on my present mount, I suggested I would like to change to another horse. He vetoed this proposition, instructing me to ride the horse I was on and, furthermore, to get back to camp by the next night or kill the horse trying to do so. Just how closely I came to filling that order was evident as I rode into the 9 9 9 Ranch next evening.

The first twenty miles or more on this trip were over a sandy-bottomed trail, suited exactly to a fractious horse who seemed to want to run, and as a result that bronc just touched the high spots. Leaving Lance Creek, I crossed a hogback onto Old Woman Creek, and after another long fast run, I came to Hat Creek Store. Feeding my mount and allowing him to rest a bit, I picked up those eighteen miles to Lusk, reaching the place during the late afternoon.

I stabled my horse and attended to business first, then spent some time with former friends and acquaintances. By daylight next morning I was on the trail heading for camp, which would have moved twenty-five miles further along toward the railroad.

Riding in at the 9 9 9 late that evening, I found my mount wasn't dead, but I was positive he'd be of no further use in a cow outfit. The 9 9 9 Ranch keeper filled me full of chuck; then, provided with a fresh horse, I rode out in the darkness, hunting camp and finding it at eleven o'clock that night. All except night guard were rolled in their blankets, while most of the boys were snoring and snorting. Locating Jim's bed, I told him his order had been filled in every particular, and I had ridden a 9 9 9 horse to camp. Now I found my own bed, unrolled it, and climbed in.

At daylight next morning the herd was thrown on the trail, and they were kept moving until we could see the smoke from the railroad. In due time they were penned and loaded; then presently they were shuffling along the Northwestern Railroad toward Chicago. No time was devoted to visiting around Chadron, but the outfit made ready to return home, and it was at this time Jim gave me his last official order.

I was to go alone to a distant ranch and get two green broncs which I was to lead home, a distance of seventy miles. This was a two-man job, yet I said nothing about it but started out to obey the order. One of those forty men should have gone along with me, yet none did; they just idled along the trail with the outfit.

In passing through a strange country, I became lost and never did find the ranch. But for one night I slept out on the prairie with the ground for a mattress, the sky for covering, and the bridle reins tied around my wrist as I had no desire to be left helpless out in that waste of country.

Before reaching the nearest ranch, I had been thirty hours without food. All during this absurd trip, my mind was in a whirl while there were brainstorms galore. By the time I reached the ranch, my mind was made up just what was going to happen. All the tough experiences passed through on this trip I'll pass over. Suffice it to say I reached the home ranch several hours ahead of the outfit, but I was tired, worn, and cranky. Dropping down on a spare bed, I fell into a profound slumber, from which I was wakened by Jim several hours later. He seemed surprised, and asked how I did it.

"Got lost while trying to find that ranch. Gave it up and headed for the ranch as I'm in a hurry to get started east," I replied.

"Quitting?" Jim asked.

"Not exactly! I quit while bunking out there on the prairie without a bed."

Jim asked me to put the blacksmith work in shape, as the year's work was finished anyway, and he'd furnish me horseflesh to go to Lusk. I realized he held the whip hand, and it was only fair to him that I should do this even though he'd played very unfair to me. Within a day or two I had the work cleaned up, and presently I was piking along toward Lusk. Upon reaching this small frontier town, I disposed of my horses as directed; then I was ready for my train east.

Never again was I to throw my leg over another AU7 horse; neither was I to take another order from Jim although I was to ride the best horses in the country and to do top work until I grew tired of it. Through the three summers I had worked for Jim, I had never received an invitation to carve, lead a drive, or represent on the outside. However, I had always commanded top wages to which I was entitled.

Presently the train whistled in; then I mounted the covered cars headed toward Iowa. Landing in Des Moines first, I sought out a good bed ground and bedded down for some needed rest. As I wandered off the bed ground next morning, I milled around through a lot of small canyons where I hoped to find wonderful sights and to meet with adventure. I didn't find either, but I did find Iowa's capital.

The principal thing I found in the city was the fact that I attracted too much attention, garbed and unshaven as I was, and I entered a barber shop and cleaned up a bit. I next visited a clothier, and on emerging from that place I might have looked like a native had it not been for those perfectly good boots I had paid Mr. Storey seven dollars for and that good Stetson felt hat which cost me six dollars.

Growing tired of milling through those small canyons, I climbed on a train and headed for home, sixty miles to the southeast. While riding along on this jerk-water train, I remembered my unknown correspondent lived in the town called Knoxville through which the train passed. This was my big chance, and when the train reached Knoxville, I dismounted and climbed on a bus. While on the way to a campground, I asked the driver if he happened to know a family by the name of —————?

"I know every man, woman, and child in this town, but none of that name," he replied.

Reaching the hotel, I put the same question up to the hotel clerk and met a similar answer. "Waterloo for me!" I thought. Now I remembered the post office and hotfooted for the place. Approaching the general delivery window, I asked for mail, giving my correct name. This brought a smile from the sickly young man on the other side, who told me he had no mail but he did have some information I wanted. He invited me to the private compartment and informed me how he had conducted the correspondence, who the young miss was, and where she lived. It seemed she had been writing to me under an assumed name; also she was a high school girl and a member of one of the first families of the town. He said she was as full of romance and adventure as a dog was full of fleas.

One thing I knew about that young miss, she was going to get a shock, and she was going to get it the first thing after I'd had supper. Now this young man asked many questions about cowboys, Indians, road agents, and bad men in general. I kept him on the ragged edges with my lies for half an hour before returning to the bed ground.

After the evening feed I started out to find a large, white house with a white picket fence around it, also a lot of green grass, shrubs, and trees. Right now I ran into the hardest proposition, as my feet wouldn't track right. At every cross street those feet wanted to turn the corner, and it required will power and determination to keep on in the right direction.

Presently the white house, picket fence and all, came in sight; then it was a real job to keep going right. To add to my difficulties, two young ladies and a young man came out of the house; the larger of the two ladies and the young man entered a buggy and drove away, leaving the other girl swinging on the gate.

If there was anything I needed worse than an alibi I can't remember it, as I was dead scared of that strip of a girl hanging on the gate, watching the others drive away. I would rather have faced a stampeding herd of cattle or ridden the worst outlaw on the ranch than face that girl. Yet I was there for that purpose, and it must be done. Despite my timidness I approached the gate and the girl and in a husky voice asked if she happened to be the individual I was looking for.

With an attitude of surprise, she stepped from the gate, squared around and looked at me, and right then she felt like stampeding. She continued gazing at yours truly; then she gave me a little smile, cackled, and informed me she was. She declared she knew who I was, but she wasn't expecting me. Anyway, I must come right in the house as we had a lot of things to talk about.

On entering the house I took a seat on one side of the room while she did likewise on the other, and for the life of me I couldn't think of a thing to say. Leave it to that girl to say things. In two minutes she was bombarding me with questions, faster than replies came. Presently we were sitting on the couch with our heads together looking at the family album.

In reply to many questions, I related desperate experiences with Indians, cow thieves, and bad men who'd as soon kill a man as look at him. I spoke of the lone freighter, and the things the Indians did to him. So interested she became in my guff she almost forgot to breathe, which demonstrated to me that this girl was a live, red-blooded American girl and interested in Western life. In this connection I will confess, I drew largely on my imagination while composing letters written to her, and now I must lie my way out of several situations she wanted to know about.

After a time I became tired of this talk and, giving the piano a look, asked her if she would play and sing for me. She seated herself at the instrument and pawed those keys to beat the band; then presently she began to sing, and believe me, she performed like a professional, only she'd stop in the middle of a song and ask some fool question about cowboys or road agents.

After a time her sister returned and I was duly introduced, but after a short visit she retired from the room, and this was the only evidence I saw that the little miss had any folks. I hung on until ten when I thought I should cut the visit and started to leave. The miss followed me to the gate, where another hour was spent in saying nothings. When I did leave her, I found it as difficult to leave that gate and white picket fence as it had been to approach it.

My unknown had been met, and she proved to be a fine American girl, plumb full of romance and deviltry and very much alive. During the passage of almost half a century I never had the pleasure of meeting this girl again, and probably I never will. Yet if she got half as much kick out of the visit as I did, she'll remember all about the green-looking cow-puncher.

Next morning I mounted a train for Albia, my home-town, but after a week spent there visiting with my people, I headed for What Cheer, Iowa, and the scenes of former labors and conquests.

A Six-shooter Episode

THE GREEN GRASS and singing birds came in the spring before I was ready, yet on the heels of this spring came the desire to be away to the range as the cows, calves, horses, and punchers were calling. The fever was on me, and I must answer the call of the range.

Placing everything in order, I mounted a train and in due time landed in Lusk. Scouting around, I was able to secure two old benches which would carry me and my bed to the 4W Ranch, located some twenty miles up the Cheyenne River from the AU7 Ranch and the place I hoped to work.

One night was spent at Hat Creek with Mr. Storey, while the next two nights were spent at the AU7 Ranch. While I planned to visit at the AU7, I had no idea of working there as three years was enough for me; yet I desired to see the gang of punchers. While back in Iowa, I had planned things to suit myself, but would they work out right?

One of the first questions fired at me by the AU7 punchers was "Did you see your unknown correspondent?" Of course I did. Then I went on to tell the boys of my experiences in Knoxville, and naturally I enlarged on the transaction as I narrated the story, which made some of the punchers green as they had not been so lucky. Bedtime came, and I piled into my bed and enjoyed a long night's refreshing sleep.

While at breakfast next morning, I was asked if I was

riding AU7 horses this year. To this question I gave an eva-
sive answer as I proposed to let Jim speak of this thing if
anything was said. The second morning while smoking and
visiting in the bunkroom, I remarked that I must be jollying
along up the river before I wore out my welcome.

This proved a shock to the gang. Even Jim got nervous.
It seemed taken for granted that I belonged to this outfit and
would hole up with them. Several punchers spoke up and
asked if I wasn't working with them this year.

"No!" I replied. "I rather think not; besides, I've had no
invitation."

At this point Jim asked if I would make some repairs for
him at the shop, and then I had an idea what was coming.
He doubtless had been thinking of lame work horses, loose
tires on the roundup wagons, and broken branding irons. As
we entered the shop, Jim bluntly asked if I wasn't going to
stick to them. Then he spoke of a perfectly good string of
horses and the same wages I had been drawing.

This sounded attractive, but to do my best I couldn't
forget that blizzard down on the Cheyenne River, nor those
two rides which would have made Paul Revere's ride look
like ten cents, to say nothing of the smallness of Phil Sheridan's short run of twenty miles. As the experience of the
past three summers flashed through my mind, I had no stomach to try another. However, I told Jim that the proposition
had been in my mind, but I had decided to try some other
outfit. Furthermore, working in the same outfit too long,
one might get to thinking he owned it, or it couldn't get
along without him, and this wouldn't promote harmony.

After the noon meal, I packed my bed on my pack horse
and piked along up the river as far as the OS Ranch. Here I
spent the night and had a fine visit with the punchers. The
boys had been holed up on the ranch all winter and were
thirsting for outside news, and believe me, I gave them an
earful. Curt Spaugh offered me a string of horses for the
summer, yet I was forced to decline them, as it would be

almost the same as working in the AU7 outfit, and I told Curt so.

Next morning I poked along the trail up the river with the 4W as my objective. I struck a moderate gait, which landed me at the 4W just before noon. At this ranch, Billy Keating had segregated about him something like forty husky punchers, all chuck full of deviltry. I knew personally most all of these men, and it will be remembered that Billy's wife claimed to be a relation to me. This was the place I had decided to work and now I was here for that purpose though up to this time I didn't know what Billy thought about it. But I would in a few moments.

As I rode up to the stable, the gang stood waiting, all curious to know who the visitor was. Billy recognized me and commenced his everlasting joshing. He desired to know where I stole those old crowbaits and what I expected to do with them. In fact, Billy was full of slanderous remarks as a dog is full of fleas. Yet despite his vile remarks, I kept my mouth shut until I finished unpacking and unsaddling.

Disposing of my mounts, I acknowledged that my horses were on their last legs, but as this trip had come to an end, I didn't give a rap what became of them as I was expecting to ride 4W horses this year. While I knew they were a bum lot of horses, they could be no worse than I had been accustomed to riding for three years.

Billy had no comeback and had to square himself before that gang of punchers by declaring my name had been on the payroll since March the first. This stumped the gang as there wasn't a man in the country who knew whether I would ever be back. I didn't know myself until the fever struck me. Within half an hour after arriving, I had unpacked my horses and landed a job in a crack outfit with a man who was as square a shooter as ever straddled a bronc.

The first unusual thing to attract my attention about the punchers, and Billy as well, was that they wore long hair though they were cleanly shaven. I learned that this was due to the fact that no man in the outfit could cut hair or would try to. It was impossible to resist poking some fun at the gang about the "House of David" and its longhaired disciples, but it would have been better for me if I had kept quiet.

While consuming the noon meal the punchers were jolly, and many were the questions asked about experiences back in the States. By this time my story was well learned, and I rehashed it for the last time. Bum as it was, it proved interesting to those thirsty punchers. With this meal finished, we retired to the bunkroom for a visit and a smoke, yet I couldn't get used to those boys and their long hair. Then pretty quick something happened. A big burly puncher came in the room with a pair of sheep shears in his hand and requested that I cut his hair. He apologized for the sheep shears by saying they were the only thing on the ranch that would cut hair, outside of the axe out on the woodpile.

I told this ferocious cowboy that I had never cut hair, couldn't cut hair, and didn't think I would try, but Billy could do the job. Still he was insistent while I just as stubbornly refused to cut hair until I felt some hard substance poking into my ribs. Then I was told to cut hair; otherwise, I'd soon be craving admission of St. Peter at the Pearly Gates.

One good look at that long hog leg, then at the puncher's face, convinced me I could cut hair. I informed this vicious puncher that while I was not afraid to die, I did think I was entirely too young, so I reckoned I'd cut hair. A whoop went up from that gang of punchers that even old Sam Groves at the Fiddleback Ranch up the river could hear.

I invited the gunman to jump astride a log out in the yard; then, to add to my humiliation, the punchers began to razz me. But wait a minute. My time was approaching. Quickly I'd have those bloodthirsty punchers dodging like cow horses. Throwing a slicker over the outlaw's shoulders, I started in with the sharp-pointed instrument of torture by crowding as much hair into them as they would hold; then I'd shut down on the handles, and it was marvelous how the dirty locks would fall to the ground.

After several trips across the calvarium, the fine work

would commence, and I'd clip each individual hair as closely to the scalp as was possible, and occasionally a small hunk of scalp would come along with the hair. This was the exciting cause of much squirming and twisting and not a little complaining.

Just the same, I was boss of the situation, and my wrath was fierce when they wouldn't hold still and take their punishment. Presently the first man was finished, and his bean reminded one of an ostrich egg. He was consoled by my telling him I could have done a better job if he had kept quiet.

To placate me, several punchers grew hysterical about the fine job I did. Perhaps they thought it would save a few notches in their scalp. Inasmuch as I had made a start, I pushed the work along with considerable speed, notwithstanding that I inflicted considerable punishment. It almost became a riot to see who would be next, so anxious were these boys to rid themselves of those dirty locks of wool.

Billy was the last man, and being a game little Irishman, he leaped astride the log and told me to dig in. By this time I had become rather expert with those large sheep shears, and it was remarkable how those locks of dirty red hair fell to the ground. No! Billy wouldn't have dodged if I had cut off an ear; however, he hung tight to the log and took his medicine.

Now that the epidemic of hair cutting was over, the heads of those punchers looked cleaner, if not better, and they resembled the aforesaid ostrich eggs, only one was unable to segregate them. At any rate, the boys had the satisfaction of knowing there wasn't a hair between them and heaven. With the work completed, the boys extended a vote of thanks although many of them had deep niches in their scalp.

Representing

THE TIME CAME for parceling horses, and when the drawing was over, it was found I had nine head to my credit, two of which were switchtails. These are horses which will violently wring their tails while running, made to do so by some nervous puncher who had constantly gouged them with his spurs.

I was told that I had drawn two good carvers, to me an indication that I would be doing some top work pretty soon. In due time we were trailing toward the roundup ground, and on looking over our bunch of men, I thought they were a peppy bunch. It seemed that a different spirit prevailed in this outfit, and for this very reason it was a most desirable place to work.

When we reached the starting place, the country proved strange to me, yet this cut no figure with experienced punchers, as anyone in our outfit would have faced the Sahara Desert and thought nothing about it. The third morning of the roundup thirty of us were chasing over a long sagebrush flat when my mount plunged both front feet into a badger hole, which cause him to turn a flip-flop while I went skyrocketing over his head. The boys halted in their mad race and congregated about me, while the older men examined my leg for broken bones.

I became faint for a short time but presently snapped back

though the pain was severe. Finding no broken bones, the boys helped me on my horse, and with a puncher for company I returned to camp. The 4W cook proved a sensible fellow, and at once he heated water and soused my sore leg with hot cloths, which helped a lot.

Billy, like all oldtime foremen, had learned a treatment which was paramount, yet in my case it did no good, but instead did do a lot of harm, as riding only aggravated the hurt. Notwithstanding this fact, he placed me on day herd and kept me there until I confessed my leg was all right. After my having confessed, Billy smiled, perhaps at the success of his treatment, then ordered me to tie my bed on a pack horse and cut out my string of horses as I was to represent on a roundup working down Running Water.

It was one glorious feeling that percolated down my spine as Billy delivered that order. Now after punching cows for three years, I had been selected from a bunch of good men to represent a good outfit on an important roundup. I congratulated Billy on his excellent judgment in selecting a man for that roundup, which caused a ripple of merriment to go through the bunch much to his embarrassment.

This roundup was to start at the Van Tassel Ranch[1] on Running Water and work down that stream to the old Sidney Stage Crossing in Nebraska. Several outfits on this roundup were sending reps to the Running Water roundup, and as a matter of convenience we bunched our horses and made the trip together. We planned to make some ranch for the night so that our horses could be corralled and fed while the ranch tender could feed us. Reaching the roundup, we put in with the OW outfit, who had a wagon on this roundup. This outfit at the time was managed by Addison Spaugh, but later the outfit passed into the hands of John B. Kendrick, now U. S. Senator from Wyoming. We continued working with this outfit until the close of the roundup.

Eastern Wyoming and western Nebraska were God's precious gift to cattle, and it was a sad time for the cattle industry when this country was despoiled by the settler and the cattle industry driven out. The settlers located along the streams of water, and they not only fenced all the streams and water holes, but their plows destroyed a lot of the best range that ever lay outdoors.

To us punchers it looked like starvation business for the settlers, and if they did partially starve, it was their hard luck. To us common punchers it seemed that the country would have served a more useful purpose had it been left as it was.

We worked with the OW to the end of the roundup, then returned to their ranch, where our cattle were cut out and we drove them to the home range. Turning our cattle loose on the home range, we pulled in at the 4W Ranch for a cleanup and a night's sleep. We started out early next morning in search of the roundup we had left some weeks before. We located it during the afternoon, and once more we became just common waddies, who must do our turn at night guard and day herd as usual.

It happened two days later that I was helping to hold the roundup in company with Frank Laberteaux, the Hoe foreman. I had recently become acquainted with Mr. Laberteaux, who enjoyed the reputation not only of being a fine fellow to work for, but of running the best outfit in the country; when a man became annexed to a job in this outfit, it required either death or a shooting match to pry him loose from his job.

"How'd you like to ride Hoe horses?" this guy asked me as we were resting our horses and he gave my mount a critical look.

"Cut it out!" I told Mr. Laberteaux as I had an idea he was making fun of my mount. "I've never seen any 4W men walking, have you?"

"No! I can't say that I have," he said, taking on a serious look. "The fact is, I have a rattling good string of horses, and they need a rider. If you want the job, bring your bed and put in with us after the works are over." Then he rode to a distant part of the herd with a grin spread over his face.

The Hoe Ranch was located on Powder River, and while

it wasn't a large outfit, there were no better outfits in the country. I knew personally that there were no better horses on the roundup than Hoe horses, and it was said this foreman was as square a shooter by his men as could be found. I did learn that he showed no favoritism to any man. When I was once located in his outfit, I could readily see how it was. He could have his pick of men, and just now I happened to be his choice. For once in my life I was to ride horses second to none and live on the fat of the land. However, on reaching the Hoe Ranch, I was to learn that Frank Laberteaux needed me worse than I needed him. Upon riding into camp at the finish of work, I told Billy I had a chance to ride Hoe horses and thought I would like to try them.

"So would I if I could get the same money for it," he replied; then he made my check for wages due and lifted my bed on the horse. I rode over to the Hoe camp, dumped my bed, and unsaddled the horse while the 4W wranglers chased it into the 4W bunch. Now I was a Hoe man and subjected to Mr. Laberteaux's orders. The Hoe punchers, several of whom I knew, gave me a nice welcome and invited me to make myself at home.

Presently Jack Bolin, that famous Hoe cook, called supper. To my surprise the punchers didn't fall over themselves to reach the dutch ovens, but all seemed unconcerned. Upon looking into those hot ovens, it occurred to me that this must be an especial occasion, yet I found all the other meals prepared much the same as this first one. This cook seemed to have several ways of cooking the same things and in such ways that one would not tire of the food. After this first meal, I didn't wonder that punchers would throw a spasm when invited to work in this outfit.

After supper the punchers roped night horses; in the meantime Frank dropped his rope over the neck of a chunky buckskin and instructed me to ride him as a night horse. He remarked that Buck could carve a little in a pinch, yet he thought the horse wrongly named as he couldn't move fast

enough to buck off a saddle blanket. After I had tried him,
I could turn him back if I didn't like the horse.

Next morning my new boss roped a large horse, which
must have weighed fourteen hundred and was so tall that it
would require a step ladder to mount him. He said the horse
was just a fair circle horse, but he would probably bring me
back to camp, if I could stick on him.

Being a runt of a kid, I looked at that horse and wondered
how I would get my saddle on him. Even if I did saddle him,
how in the world would I mount him without help? After a
time, the seemingly impossible was accomplished, and I was
sitting on top of the world, or at least the most powerful
circle horse on the roundup. Never during my cowpunching
days did I experience the feeling I now enjoyed. I was as well
or better mounted than any man on the roundup, and now
I need not eat any man's dust as I always did while riding
AU7 horses.

Now, it occurred to me, would be a good time to show
someone how it felt to eat dust and to square off some old
accounts. The man in question was called on to lead a long
drive, and I made it my business to get off on this drive;
furthermore, it was my business to circumvent him and see
that he should be dropped off while I must ride in the lead.

Mounted on this Herculean horse I was able to ride in the
lead of the leader all the way around the circle, yet my work
was done as well as it could be done. To me it was a rare
treat to watch that leader spur and quirt his horse, trying to
get in the lead, but it couldn't be done, and I doubt that he
had a horse in this outfit that could have done it.

As the circle became small, and all the men were with the
herd, I remarked to this leader what a long, hard drive it had
been, especially when one wasn't well mounted. He grunted
and gave me a killing look and rode to another part of the
herd.

Upon reaching camp, I found all hands enjoying Jack's
good dinner, and while I was hungry and thirsty, I was

enjoying a situation that couldn't have fitted into my scheme
of things better. Furthermore, I knew that during the work
I might possibly have another chance to do a little carving,
and if so there might be some fun.

Frank grinned and said nothing as he had his hunch what
I had been up to, and to me it just naturally seemed like I
owed a debt of gratitude to someone for making this thing
possible.

---

[1]Quite probably the ranch of R. S. Van Tassell. An early rancher, Van
Tassell was one of the original group of five men who met in Cheyenne
in 1872 to organize a vigilance committee to deal with rustling in the area.
These meetings were the first step toward formation of the Wyoming
Stock Growers Association. See *Cow Country Cavalcade*, p. 40.

In Clover

CATCH BUCK! said Frank. "He's good about the roundup."
Without waste of time I had Buck under the saddle,
and we were on our way to the roundup ground. The foreman pointed out a herd to Frank, and instead of leaving me
on the outside to hold the herd as had been the usual thing,
he invited me to help him cut cows and calves. Before we
had run out the first cow and calf, I found Buck was a go-
getter, even as good as the black streak of lightning at Chugwater.

I was ready to dismount and take off my hat to Buck,
and from this time until I quit the outfit, if anyone had said
a disrespectful word about Buck, he'd have had an argument
on his hands. The work went forward with a snap, and it
was marvelous how Buck could move. Now there was no
grabbing the saddle horn, neither any pulling leather or flop-
ping stirrups, but I could ride a cow horse as well as anyone.
In contrast, my only experience carving during my first three
years was to dodge one out from the edge of the milling herd.

While working this herd another outfit rode up and waited
until we finished; then they'd work the bunch and follow us
to the next one. I decided it would be a good time to create
some further excitement and started to do so.

Now we were working single, cutting out dry stuff, and
I adopted a style of carving I had seen practiced for three

165

years, which called forth considerable merriment. Most every man has his peculiar way of carving, and to watch some men, it would cause one to think the fellow was trying to show off as I was about to do.

While all the men enjoyed my antics to a limited extent, there was one man who certainly did not, yet what could he do about it? The outstanding feature about my good horses was the fact that I was given a chance to use them. It seemed that some foreman in the country had watched my work and had appreciated my efforts.

Frank kept me working in the herd until we had finished the work while this other outfit had followed us all the way around. Now I was getting my chance, doing the work that punchers liked to do. For three long summers I had longed and thirsted to do this top work, yet I had never received an invitation; my activities were confined to holding the herd while the other fellow did the carving. However, I had the consolation of receiving the largest wages of them all except the foreman.

After a few more days of work, the roundup came to an end, and the outfits pointed their herds toward their home ranges. Our herd was pointed west toward the Powder River divide, and after two days we turned loose in the river breaks. With the herd off our hands, we pulled in at the horse camp on the divide near Pumpkin Buttes and made camp for the night.

This completed the early part of the summer's work, and after turning our horses out on the range, we rolled out our beds for a long undisturbed night's rest. We slept late next morning, for the simple reason that we didn't have to get up. After a hearty breakfast, we headed out over those twenty miles of the worst badlands I'd ever seen. As a bird would fly, it was said to be ten miles to the ranch on the river, yet as our trail led to the place, it proved twenty long miles.

I wondered afterward how we ever negotiated those twenty miles without going into the ditch and being all smashed to pieces, yet we landed at the ranch and nothing happened. After we left the horse camp, our trail led over the extreme heights of the divide where a panorama spread out before me, the like of which in point of grandeur I never saw before or since, notwithstanding that I have traveled over forty-two states.

There, seemingly but a stone's throw away to the west, loomed the most majestic range of mountains I ever expect to see. Those Big Horn Mountains, with their snowcapped peaks projecting far above the clouds, sparkled like diamonds in the morning sunshine. Resting my horse on the summit of this high elevation, I feasted my eyes and mind on one of the grandest pictures Nature has to show.

Up to the margin of the low-hanging clouds, the mountain sides were a dark green while the clouds obstructed the timber line as they hung lazily on the mountain side without a breath of wind to disturb them. Sloping down from the base of the mountains, the country was made up of a series of smaller mountains merging into hills as they approached the river. Through these hills one was able to trace mountain streams as they came out of the mountains and found their way to the parent stream. Above the clouds projected those snowcapped peaks, rounding out the most wonderful picture.

The country between the divide and the river was made up of thousands of gullies, sharp pinnacles, and hogbacks, presenting the most chopped-up ground I ever saw. The country presented an appearance as though it had suffered from an avalanche which was responsible for its present condition.

Powder River, seen from my point of vantage, presented an appearance resembling a mighty reptile winding its serpentine way to the southwest and disappearing into the mountains that marked the skyline. The narrow valley was covered with a dense growth of trees, lending a coloring to the barren hills which was marvelous. To the north, the river ran almost straight north as far as vision would carry. The

This photograph is inscribed in Mullins's handwriting: "Taken in Wyoming on the AU7 Cow Ranch in 1885—R.B. Mullins." *Photo courtesy of Maxine Mullins.*

adjacent country seemed hilly and barren, yet as it passed toward the east it flattened out into a prairie country.

To the south, four buttes stood in a row from north to south, separated from each other by two miles. They were located on the summit of the divide, which caused them to be seen many miles away, and they served travelers as a useful landmark. The tops of these buttes seemed level one with another, and it caused me to believe that in the distant past this had been the surface of the country.

Toward the southeast one could see the origin of Belle Fourche Creek, in the midst of a country I would have called Paradise. On inquiry, I was told the Rockies were fully seventy miles from where I rested, yet it looked but a stone's throw. Long ago I found that in this country vision carried much further than it did a few hundred miles east. I know I was often fooled in the distance to a known point.

As we pulled up at the river on this trip through the dense timber in the river bottom, I received my second shock that day. Just across the river on the other bank, I saw a beautiful, white frame house with picket fence and all other buildings to match. I needed only to close my eyes and visualize some nice farm home back in Iowa. Yet after an inside look, I found this place very much of a cow ranch with its wood stove, spit boxes, and homemade chairs and table. Yet it differed from other cow ranches, inasmuch as there were iron bedsteads and springs. However, after one night spent on those springs, I moved my bed out on the ground where I could sleep with comfort and ease.

From past experiences I was led to believe that all cow ranches were the same: that is, built of logs and chinked and daubed in the cracks between the logs, which bred bedbugs by the barrel. Personally I would select cooties anytime as bedfellows rather than bedbugs.

Powder River was narrow, but deep with steep banks. The bottom of the stream was as a rule mirey. It was said a saddle blanket would sink into the mire. Experience taught me that this river would fill with water in a few hours then as quickly run dry. While running full, it looked a dangerous stream, and before I left the country, I was to have my experience with it.

Shortly we were across the river and not an accident to our credit. The wagons were pulled up near the ranch and unloaded, and after once becoming organized, we rested.

New Friends

AFTER TWO DAYS' resting I became restive and made a trip of exploration. This trip landed me at what I thought was a blacksmith shop. It was a fine little frame building, all painted white, and when I poked my head in the door, I found it very much a blacksmith shop with a nice set of tools but badly shot due to some greenhorn trying to do blacksmith work. I also found real blacksmith coal, and in a few moments I had the fire burning on the forge and the anvil ringing.

Shortly after I got started placing the tools in shape for work, Frank poked his face in at the door with a Cheshire cat smile all over his face and asked what all the racket meant when a fellow needed sleep. "Jack said it couldn't be done, but I had an idea I could work you. Never did see a fellow fall so easily."

"Cut out the guying and get those lazy punchers to pull that old mowing machine to the shop," I told this boss.

"Hot dog!" howled Frank. "It was what I wanted done, but I didn't have the guts to ask you just yet." Then he hotfooted it for the ranch. Shortly the machine was at the shop, and I went carefully over it.

Other than greasing the machine and tightening up a few bolts, the machine was ready for the hay field. This job of cutting hay was turned over to George Wellman, Frank's underboss, under whose supervision the work went forward to a conclusion.

Mr. Laberteaux took up his residence in the shop and after a little training developed into a very good helper. This blacksmith work was paramount with Frank, and it seemed he proposed to stay right with me until the work was finished. The bed and mess wagons were placed in repair first as they had reached the stage where they were unfit for further work. Work horses came in for a shoeing while broken branding irons were scattered about the place in profusion.

By the time the haymaking was finished, we had the mechanical work completed; then I had a siege with broken spurs, bridle bits and old six-shooters. Hardly had I got through with the punchers when here came Jack Bolin with a crude drawing in his fist. He explained that it was a device to protect his fire from wind and rain while cooking on the roundup. Jack declared he had for years been trying to find someone who could make the contraption, but so far he had failed.

Looking over his sketch and receiving his explanation, I could see there was nothing to it so far as mechanical ingenuity was concerned. Well, I knew roundup cooks, and I further knew they were a mighty good lot of fellows to stand in with as they could slip a hungry puncher a handout 'most any time. With this idea in view, I sailed into Jack's fire protector while Jack stuck right to me, only leaving the shop long enough to cook his meals. Finally the job was completed, causing Jack to give a howl of delight as he surveyed the product. Right then I had a hunch I need not ever go hungry if Jack Bolin was around.

Frank stuck to the shop as long as any work could be found, but he finally acknowledged we were through. With all his joking, he had proven a good helper and a congenial companion, and he was always up and coming. However, there was a quiet dignity about the fellow that commanded respect. He was one among those foremen who didn't pose as "I'm better than thou," but he was considerate of his men. When he gave an order, it was done more in the form of a request, yet the puncher understood he meant just what he said and he must be prompt to obey.

While smoking and resting in the bunkroom a day later, I found I had been the object of a conspiracy and was a doomed man. It came about through a man who was a stranger to me, who had ridden in at the ranch and housed himself up with Frank in his den. Presently I was to learn that this stranger was to be the cause of my doing a lot of work and losing a lot of sweat.

After some time, Frank stepped into the bunkroom and invited me to enter his Sanctum Sanctorum to meet Al Sproul, foreman of the 21 Ranch, five miles up Powder River. Upon entering Frank's den, I gave the stranger the once over, and I noticed he had coal black eyes which constantly snapped. He was tall and slender with bowlegs due to a lifetime spent in the saddle.

To offset those snappy eyes, he had a most pleasing manner and voice. Directing his conversation to me, he opened up by saying that everything on the 21 Ranch was shot to pieces, and if his men attended another roundup, his outfit would have to have help such as I could give them. The tires on the wagon wheels were held on by wire while other parts were held together by means of rawhide thongs. Just what to do was a problem as blacksmiths were as scarce as chicken's teeth. He had talked over the situation with Mr. Laberteaux, who was willing that I should help them out if it suited me. He would be more than glad to pay me well for the service.

This man seemed so nice about his troubles, and I had sensed the fact that he and Frank were warm friends; then I learned that the two outfits worked together, much the same as the OS and the AU7, so I consented to help this distracted cowpuncher out of a hole.

Frank had sat quietly waiting the outcome of the interview, but now he snapped back and had the boys pack my bed on a horse and saddle another for me. Mr. Sproul and I piked along toward the 21 Ranch. This 21 outfit was new to me. I didn't know a man in the outfit, yet that didn't prevent their giving me a nice welcome. All realized just what my work meant to the outfit and to them.

Upon entering their shop, I could readily see the condition had not been exaggerated, for things were badly shot. The tools seemed ruined, and broken branding irons were strewn everywhere about the shop and ranch. Pitching into the tools first, I sweated half a day on them, then started in on the main job with Mr. Sproul as helper. [Working steadily, we managed to get the work done in time for the next drive.]

Salt Creek

SOON WE WERE OUT on the trail heading up the river for the mouth of Salt Creek, now the most famous oil field in the world. Coming up to the 21 Ranch, which set back close to the river, we found the outfit out on the trail waiting as from this point we would mingle and visit.

Once we reached the campground, the tents were pitched close together at the mouth of Salt Creek and under the shadows of the Big Horn Mountains. The place looked romantic and a most delightful camping place. However, we would find the romantic part coming to us next day in great hunks.

First thing I did on reaching camp was to roll out my bed and flop down on it, bent on getting a lot of sleep. Soon I fell into a profound slumber and slept until I was wakened by two men laughing in a tent close at hand. Yes, it was Frank and Al, perhaps having a laugh at my expense. However, I didn't give a rap, but turned over and went to sleep and continued sleeping until Jack called supper.

With the meal finished, the boys staged a war dance, and all the fool hopping and jigging around the campfire with their ki-yi's would cause any dead Indian to turn over in his grave and groan. I sat quietly on my bed and watched the mutts for a time then crawled down deep between my blankets.

Already I had been told about Salt Creek and what we must face on driving the country, and that I must fortify myself for that inferno which the country was supposed to be. Cowpunchers who knew Salt Creek didn't approve of it as a cow country, and after my first drive had been made, it would cause a shudder to pass over me when I thought of the place.

All water holes, creeks, and other sources of water were contaminated with oil. In places, the oil could be seen floating on the surface of water holes. Were some puncher thirsty and brave enough to take a drink from some water hole, it tasted of oil, and why any sensible cow would remain in such a country, no one knew.

To make this particular drive, each puncher caught his toughest and strongest circle horses, and when the time came, all were rearing to get off on the drive and have the agony over. Both Al and Frank rode their best circle horses, and they lit out at a dangerous speed over the rottenest piece of country I ever helped drive.

After a long hard run, the horses were pulled in and allowed to rest while the punchers smoked. By this time Old Sol had commenced to do business, and the higher it rose in the sky, the hotter it became until it got so hot it almost set our clothes on fire. With a condition like this existing and no water to drink for man or horse, it was awful!

At one o'clock we drove our herd onto the roundup ground, and it was a mad race to camp where we gulped down pails of water that stood in the shade waiting. With water and food, we soon reached the stage where we could smile. Without doubt this was the worst short experience I had had while punching cows; yet if I remained in this outfit I would make this drive about three times each summer.

Mounted on fresh horses and our stomachs full, we speedily forgot Salt Creek as we took up our work. The very first thing, Al invited me to help cut cows and calves, and to me it was evident he'd started in to get square. Evidently Mr.

Sproul knew what punchers liked to do most, and from this time until I quit the range, it was do top work until I grew tired of it. If it wasn't Al, it was Frank who'd invite me to carve, even over the heads of older and better men. With all this favor shown me, it seemed to leave no sore spots as the punchers had appreciated what my help had meant to both outfits.

The Salt Creek drive netted a large bunch of calves, and presently the branding operation was in full swing. However, with that hot sun beating down and the condition aggravated by the large fire, combined with much activity of all the punchers, a condition was created equal to an inferno.

A half hour after we got going, who should undertake to make us a visit but a large diamond rattler. This old scout crawled out to the center of the branding pen, coiled up in a neat pile, raised his head from the center of the same, poked out his tongue, and shook his tail in defiance of the punchers. Now anyone who knew punchers and their method of handling such guests will know that a pistol cracked, and the spirit of that rattler passed into the land of its ancestors, leaving his beautiful carcass behind to be skinned by some lusty puncher who wanted that hide for a hatband. I halted my activities long enough to examine that carcass, which looked to be a clear pink meat; yet it created no desire on my part for a roast. At the completion of the work an hour later, the rattler was kicked onto the red coals, only to squirm and twist as though it were alive.

Rattlers caused the loss of both cattle and horses, and I have heard of punchers getting theirs; yet from personal experience I never knew a puncher who had been bitten by a rattler. During my first year on the range I was told how a rattler crawled onto the breast of a sleeping puncher and coiled up for a nap. However, some quick work on the part of the puncher greatly disturbed the rattler's rest.

Our second day's work was over a country equally as rough as Salt Creek, yet we had an abundance of good water, and the drive wasn't half bad. As the roundup progressed down Powder River, the general contour of the country remained about the same; at times there wasn't enough level ground to whip a dog.

Despite this rough country, the roundup snapped along, and gradually I became used to this kind of riding. It was while working for the Hoe outfit that I received a couple of thrills, one of which caused gooseflesh to come. I was riding a divide, throwing down any cattle found there among the pine and cedar trees, when I received my first thrill. I was poking along looking for cattle in the gulches and pockets, not thinking of anything in particular, when my horse suddenly stopped and undertook to whirl back. Looking for the exciting cause I saw a crevice in the ground just ahead, which gave out smoke or vapor which smelled like the coal I attempted to use at the AU7 Ranch.

I went the horse one better and backed up to quite a distance, thinking it might be a latent volcano. The crevice was many yards long and fully twelve inches wide. Below this crevice the ground had a caved-in appearance, while numerous burned logs and stumps were scattered over the surface. "Burning coal mine," was my diagnosis, verified when I reached camp. I was told the Indians had reported this burning coal mine long before the first white man entered the country. I know my first contact with this burning mine caused the gooseflesh to come.

While engaged in the same work and on this same divide at a later period, my attention was attracted to something in the treetops far below me that resembled large nests. Being curious, I rode down to them, only to find small platforms in the tree tops, constructed of boughs from the dead trees bound together with rawhide thongs. Climbing a few of the trees, I found a dead Indian on each but in different stages of decomposition. As I rode away, I thought them the very best bunch of Indians I had ever seen.

It was during my time on the AU7 that a puncher reported

a find on Lance Creek which attracted considerable attention. This curio took the form of a massive upper end of a femur bone, and it projected from a clay embankment several feet. Seventeen years later, while pesticating around through the National Museum in Washington, I found my bone from Lance Creek. How did I know? Both the date and place of resurrection were labeled on the bone.

Our roundup continued on down Powder River, yet the country became no smoother until we came to where Horse Creek empties into Powder River. Occasionally during this roundup new outfits would join us, which gave an opportunity to extend one's acquaintance. The LX put in with the roundup, and I became very well acquainted with its foreman, Mr. Charles Hilderbrand. Hilda, as we called him, hit the spot with me, and he proved to be a pretty good fellow. One day while chewing the rag with him, I boned him for a saddle trade, never dreaming he would trade his Visalia saddle for my old kidney swiper.

I'll remark that at this period on the range, a Visalia saddle was the big joy of the puncher's heart and all that was necessary to make him happy. Hilda declared he'd do anything for a friend, and he reckoned he'd give me an even trade.

This offer came as a shock, yet I kept quiet, and getting a grip on myself, I invited him to ride out some distance from the cattle and we'd exchange, never dreaming he would do so. To my surprise he did come along with me, and we removed our saddles. When he drew his from the horse, it fell into three parts; then I could understand all that friend stuff.

Well, this was the place I must take a trimming, I thought, as we made the exchange; yet I couldn't help but tell him he'd taken a base advantage of my youthfulness, and he'd swipe the coppers off a dead nigger's eyes. This only caused Hilda to laugh the harder; then I did get mad, but I had to eat dirt when I was obliged to ask his help in fastening the saddle on my horse.

Charley sure did guy me that afternoon, but with all his guying, I rode carefully, fearing that both the saddle and I would fall off the horse. Upon reaching camp I received another razzing. Quickly I dived down in my war bag, and when I came out, I had my hands full of new whang leather strings. With the aid of Marlin Spike and a few of the punchers, I soon had those strings tied in the saddle, and then it was as good as new. When I pulled up alongside Hilda next day, he spotted my new strings; then he wanted to trade back. Now it was my turn to do a little guying, and I told him to take his trimming like a man.

He was very much the same type as Frank and Al, and it was through the efforts of the three that we would take the day off and rest both horses and men. After a long time we reached the Montana line; then the roundup disbanded. For me it had been a steady grind all through the summer, yet I never seemed to grow tired as when riding bum horses.

Reaching the home range, we turned loose our herd; then we made tracks for the horse camp on the divide. Here we parted from our saddle horses as usual, and after resting a day, we trailed down through those badlands to the ranch. This time there wasn't a lot of blacksmith work to be done, so I took a lot of comfort on my bed.

Before starting out on the beef roundup, Frank asked me to make a trip to the horse camp, a trip that took almost a full day. On my return to Powder River that evening, I found the river running bank-full of tumbling and muddy water which looked dangerous. Well, I wanted very much to get across that troubled stream, but as there was no bridge or ferry, I knew I must either swim across, camp where I was with no bed, or return to the horse camp through those twenty miles of badlands, none of which looked good to me.

I had never faced an experience like this one, and I'll confess the proposition didn't look good, yet something must be done about it. After deliberating a few moments, I let out a whoop that brought the punchers out of the ranch in a hurry. I had decided to swim my horse across that stream and thought the boys might as well know how it happened when we should have been across that river already; but not knowing my horse's capabilities, there was plenty of hesitation on my part.

Those Hoe punchers were accustomed to this condition and thought nothing about swimming the river, so they commenced handing out their advice. Calling back to the rotten bunch, I told them to go to a place I knew they wouldn't and made ready for my bath in the river. I removed my boots and most of my clothing; then, tying them to the saddle, I mounted my horse, slipped the bridle off his head, and it was remarkable how quickly he ducked for the water.

It was a thing the horse expected in the first place, and in a very short time we were clambering out of the water on the other side while the punchers stood by laughing at my fears. Just the same, I'll remark that it was no laughing matter with me at the time; it required more nerve than any job I ever faced.

Fighting a Prairie Fire

YES! THERE THEY WERE. The entire flock, horses and all, were out on the trail waiting for us to come up to them. Now everything was mixed but the saddle horses, and they rubbered at each other. This time it was going to be the beef roundup and a long hard pull before it was all over.

This proved to be a typical beef roundup, with its constant night guard and day herd. Some weeks later this roundup came to an end, and as a result of our work, we had six hundred head of choice beef cattle, which we had to trail over two hundred miles to the railroad.

Mr. Henry Blair, the owner of the Hoe outfit, put in with us near the close of the roundup and remained with us until we started our herd for the railway. It was said of this man that he was a banker of note in Chicago and a baseball fan. It was said further that his Hoe outfit was a side issue with him and a sport he took a lot of interest in as well as a means of making a lot of money.

Whether it was a hobby or not was a matter that did not concern us as it was the best outfit in the country to work in, and that was all that mattered with the punchers. While Mr. Blair proved a good sport while with us, he was also a good cowman. During his first evening in camp a couple of ribs were broiling on the coals, sending out a delicious aroma which caused this cattle baron to sniff; then he made a run for the puncher who was doing the broiling, and it was refreshing to watch this man beg for a stand-in on the rib.

At the conclusion of the banquet, Mr. Blair filled his pipe, and then he could tell as many rotten stories as any old puncher in the outfit. While with us, Mr. Blair would ride as hard and as far as any of his men, and he knew exactly where to cut in to make his work effective. His last evening in camp was spent riding about the herd in company with Frank, supposedly admiring those fine beef steers. Occasionally he would point to some fine specimen, and I thought they were calculating how much kale he'd bring on the market.

The fact of the matter was that Mr. Blair was not the only man who admired our fine beef herd as all of us punchers had vowed a vow that we would deliver that herd into the cars without a run to their credit. Early next morning our herd grazed off the bed ground toward distant Chadron while Mr. Blair had his drivers hitched to his buckboard and went bumping down through the badlands toward the ranch, then to Douglas and Chadron.

With our late vow in mind, every puncher was on his toes, and it was a cinch no man would do a thing to start the herd running. It was our desire that the herd should monkey along the trail and take on flesh all during the trip, but could we deliver the goods? We were betting we could. We jollied along the trail with our herd until they became too lazy and fat to run; then in due time we could see the smoke from the trains, and we went into camp.

Frank made his trip to Chadron, and arrangements were made for shipment. Returning to camp that evening, Mr. Blair accompanied Frank and seemed anxious to see his herd. Happy! Why the man almost had hysterics, and I actually believe he would have committed murder for any one of his punchers after he saw the herd. In due time the herd was loaded into the cars and on their way to Chicago, there to be converted into nice, juicy beefsteaks and served up to the American people as delicious morsels of food.

With climatic conditions good and our health fair, we had a burning desire to once more look over Chadron and note the many changes that had taken place. Now it seemed the place had become overcivilized and totally unsuited for the entertainment of cowpunchers. Now there were many fine business blocks and numerous substantial and nice homes; altogether the place had taken on an appearance of stability and permanency. The Northwestern Railroad had built shops and established a division point where many railroad men were employed, a very few of whom live in my town and are my friends at this time.

My first visit was to a clothier, where I bought a few winter duds; then I took the opportunity to doll up a bit. Not being in sympathy with drinking and gambling, I cut those places, and at a later period I found that some of our fellows had better done likewise.

Jack Bolin took the occasion to stock up on grub, and when his wagons were loaded, it was evident the Hoe punchers wouldn't go hungry for a long time. Two days spent in Chadron were the limit. Even at that some of the boys found themselves broke; yet they had bought winter clothing.

The celebrations being over, we struck the trail for Powder River. At the start we took things leisurely along the trail. However, climatic conditions changed for the worse, and we took on speed, which soon landed us at the horse camp.

The weather having cleared up, Frank decided we would make a small roundup about Pumpkin Buttes, where the country had not been worked to his satisfaction. He proved a good guesser as we caught a number of unbranded calves which would have shed their mothers by spring and then would have been mavericks.

It was dark on reaching camp from this day's work, and while unsaddling our tired horses, a bright light suddenly sprang up in the east which needed no explanation. All knew it was a prairie fire, and we hurriedly ate supper, caught fresh horses, and saddled them. Securing gunnysacks, we soaked them in water, then mounted and lit out for the fire, riding in pairs.

Even though it was dark, we rode like demons toward the fire as everyone knew it would burn over thousands of acres in a short time, which would cause the cattle to drift, perhaps far from home, in their search for food. My partner rode like a wild man while I was at his heels, and we were urging our horses to even a faster speed as we knew time was an important factor in times like this.

Coming to the fire, I was disappointed. I expected to find the flames leaping to the sky while it would be traveling over the country like a wild horse, destroying all kinds of life that obstructed its path. Instead, we found a feeble little blaze which would almost die out where the grass was short; yet this fire was capable of destroying thousands of acres of winter feed.

We dismounted and tied ropes about the necks of our horses; then, removing the bridles, we made them fast to our saddles, and business began. With our backs together, the lead rope in one hand and the wet gunnysack in the other, we commenced whipping out that line of fire, leaving no spark behind us. This was the last I saw of my buddy until in camp next morning.

Up and down went my arm until it would become so tired it felt like falling off and I felt I had to rest a few moments, then go on with my work. This continued all through the night, and should I come to a water hole, I would wet my sack, then sail into the fire once more. Just before the break of day I came to the end of the fire. Look as much as I would, I couldn't see as much as a spark; then the fight was over, but where was I?

I hadn't the faintest idea in the world where camp was, yet my horse would crane his neck in a certain direction and whinny. If I had had sense enough, I should have given the horse the rein, and we would shortly have been in camp. As it was, I retired to a hilltop, lit my pipe, and waited for daylight. Presently light did come out of the east, enabling me to locate myself, and presently we were in camp. After a big feed and a smoke, I crawled between my blankets and slept until late afternoon. When I arose from my bed that afternoon, my joints, especially my arm, had gone lame and were getting worse every minute. Next morning I was so lame and sore I could hardly mount and face those badlands. Eventually we reached the ranch, but all alike were tired and sore.

After cleaning up, we rested a week. Then one morning Frank commenced to invite us into his sanctum, and he kept us coming until each man in the outfit was fired except the cook and horse wrangler. My turn came along with the balance, and I was invited to be seated as he had a few words to say to me. He opened up by saying that while he tolerated me in the outfit, I was worthless as a puncher and was now fired. However, to keep me in the country he had secured a job for me at a granger ranch up the river where considerable blacksmith work was to be done. If I wanted the job, I must start moving as he was dead tired looking at me. In order to get out of sight quickly, I could saddle his private horse now tied in the stable and scoot. Just whether Frank wanted me to fly into a rage and give him a licking, I didn't know, but I did know that no man, not even Mr. Blair, had ever received an invitation to ride that horse. Assuming a hurt and humiliated attitude, I told this bluffer that I would try out the job, but I fully intended to return to the Hoe Ranch, and if I found that anyone had ridden little Buck, there would be a shooting match.

My speech brought on a case of hysteria Frank couldn't control. The old puncher howled loud and long, which brought the punchers into the room for investigation.

A Man with a Temper

A FTER RIDING FRANK'S road horse to the granger ranch, I did not wonder that Frank offered to bet a hundred bucks that he could single-foot the horse a hundred miles in ten hours. I knew I had never seen a horse that could knock off the miles like this one.

After reaching this granger ranch, my horses were put away, my bed placed in the small bunkhouse, and I was ready for anything, even though it was a fight. This ranch proved to be a cross between a small stock ranch and a granger farm. The boss nester met me with a patronizing smile and showed me where to dispose of my stuff; then we had a look at the shop. I will admit Frank was right as there was a lot of blacksmith work piled about. The shop was roomy and had very good tools as well as blacksmith coal.

While conversing with this man, I got an insight into his character when one of his men asked about some work. I decided on the spot it would be as well for him if he'd assume a different attitude when talking to me.

Of course the bunkhouse was small, yet it housed six men and made room for another. Even at that, very little time was spent in the bunkroom by the men as they had only a scant eight hours for refreshments and sleep, the balance of the time being devoted to work. The family consisted of the granger, his wife, two children, and a domestic, twenty years old. One side of her face was covered with a red birthmark, destroying all hope of a husband, a thing she desired very much. Six men, or slaves, worked for this man from early morn until after dark, taking all kinds of abuse in the meantime. Even at that, they would submit to a cussing with a "Yes, sir," and no back talk. Three times each day we were allowed in his house long enough to swallow food, then got out, and I thought it unfair to the domestic.

A few days after making a start, a horse was led to the shop with instruction to shoe him, and after a hard tussle with the horse, I gave up and hunted up my boss and asked for help. He replied that no one was available, and I returned to the shop for another round with this mean horse.

During the scuffle the horse wrenched my back, which caused me to break out, and the way I used my little shoeing hammer on that brute came as a surprise to him. In just a couple of minutes I had welts standing out on him, and just as the battle reached high-water mark, the boss came around the corner of the shop and, believe me, he had his nasty temper and wasn't long getting it into action.

This nester started in to do the most remarkable job of swearing I'd ever heard even while working in coal mines among miners who are past masters at cussing. The cuss words flowed so fast and smoothly I thought him an artist. However, I wasn't afraid of him or his cussing and tirade of words, but I did quit beating the horse and stood looking at him with my little hammer in my hand and a smile on my face.

Presently I started laughing at the man and the artistic way he handled the English language. This seemed to aggravate him, and he cursed harder and faster than ever. Then a strange look came into his face, and he commenced to slow down. Soon, now, he ceased to swear and proceeded to get into a good humor. But why the quick change? Maybe it was the great pile of blacksmith work waiting on my humble efforts. Anyway he became friendly, even chummy.

Now for the first time I spoke, reminding him how cold it was going to be in his shop. I told him if he'd hurry up and write my check for wages due, I'd be able to catch the first stage south to Douglas as I desired to see some friends there. He said that if I would stop with him, he would promise it wouldn't occur again, and he would raise my wages ten a month.

I told the nester it wasn't possible to stop a minute longer if I was to catch the stage, so he must please hurry with my check. In due time I was perched on top of the stage beside the driver while the horses were galloping to Douglas.

From Douglas I went to Glenrock, where I found plenty of friends. I found work at the mine during the winter, but with the coming of spring I thought of Buck and the punchers. After some maneuvering, I found myself located on the Hoe Ranch and under pay.

By this time I was getting my fill of cowpunching but was just commencing to find it out. I decided I would go through this year's work, and it would be my last. I will confess I was ambitious to do things, yet my ambition didn't run in that channel.

The Open Range Doomed

THE COMING OF railroads into the country had struck the death knell for the open range. Many large herds were being driven north in search of unrestricted range, and some were being sold. Large bands of sheep were coming into the country. Settlers were squatting along the best streams.

During the calf roundup I passed through the most dangerous experience I ever want to. We were almost to the new campground when a rumbling came down from the mountains. Just as we finished putting up our tents, the storm broke. The rain turned into hail, some of the stones as large as tomatoes. Limbs were torn from trees, and old tents were torn to shreds. There were no casualties, but there were many bruises. The horses and cattle mixed, and it was a job to untangle them. After the roundup was over, Mr. Blair put in with us and at once noticed the depression among the men. Soon his wisecracks were flying. This cheered the punchers, and presently they were as hearty as ever.

During this drive an old sage hen flew up from a clump of sagebrush and caused a steer to jump and snort, then presto! the entire herd was off, working on high. Our bunch was the one which finally stopped the stampede. In order to stop the milling, experienced men cut into the herd at different points along the flank, and presently the cattle were grazing peacefully. But for a time every man in the outfit spent most of his time in the saddle among the herd.

After loading the cattle, we were all cranky, muddy, and tired. However, Jack Bolin knew what would restore us to normal, and under his hot coffee and grub we forgot our sore spots and were able to smile. Presently, all were laughing and talking and why not? We had done our best, which was all that mortal man could do, and the results must be accepted, whether Mr. Blair or anyone else liked it or not.

With our stomachs full, we smoked as we stood before the campfire and dried our clothes. In the meantime a puncher would relate an experience he had had with some outlaw steer. Presently we crawled into our beds, bent on having a long night's undisturbed sleep. When we rose the next morning, climatic conditions were still bad and threatening to be more so.

Frank decided we'd best pick up the trail for home as there wouldn't be a bit of joy milling around Chadron in the midst of such weather. Our second day out of Chadron, climatic conditions changed for the better, and we enjoyed fine weather all through our trip home. At the horse camp, our horses were turned out on the range for the winter, and now I must say goodbye to little Buck.

Upon returning to the home ranch, we went through the same old formula of cleaning, and while doing so I was forming my line of action. The time had come to forsake the punchers, the cows, the horses, and the open range. I realized that I must enter a different world and take up an entirely different line of work, and the start must be made now.

Knocking at Frank's door, I was invited to come in, and when he saw the disturbing element he asked, "What is on your mind?"

Replying, I said, "Any young man who will punch cows for an extended number of years isn't normal. I have worked six years in cow outfits and am fed up on cow punching, so I'm quitting. In punching cows there is absolutely nothing to look forward to, other than monthly wages, doing top work, and riding good horses. Possibly in the far distant future one might become a foreman, yet that is problematical as the cow business is headed for the bow-wows, and there is not long to go, so why wait for the deluge? I have appreciated the good treatment I've received and the good horses I have ridden in the Hoe by giving the outfit my best efforts, yet the entire business has got on my nerves. I have fully decided to fall back on my trade as time is passing and I'm not getting anywhere. I feel that my passing must be delayed no longer if I expect to get anywhere during my short span of years as age is advancing regardless of personal wishes."

Frank looked serious. He knew, perhaps better than I, what havoc settlers and sheep men were creating in the cow country, and while he did not tell me to go, he did not urge me to stay.

Having settled with Frank, I decided to hold a sale and dispose of my puncher outfit, thus burning my bridges behind me. I sent word to the 21 Ranch of the time of my sale, and the entire gang rode in at the appointed time as there were several fellows in the 21 Ranch who wanted my Visalia saddle. The result of my sale was most satisfactory as the outfit netted me more cash than I had originally put into it.

With this sum of money piled on top of my summer's wages, I was very well fixed to face the world in the new environment into which I was about to plunge. With the sale concluded and the money stowed away in my inside pocket, I told the Hoe fellows goodbye and mounted a borrowed horse, riding away with the 21 boys. That afternoon was spent at the 21 discussing the past, present, and future of the open range and the vanishing cow business.

Next day the fellows took me to Powder River crossing, where the goodbyes were said once more, and I mounted the old stage coach and headed out into that big country of which I knew so little, yet which held in store so much work still to be done.

Now, forty-three years have passed. It has never been my

Dr. Reuben Mullins in Baltimore in 1905, where he was completing a year of study in dentistry. *Photo courtesy of Priscilla Hogan.*

pleasure to meet one of those men of either ranch since, and only in my mind can I visualize a visit with them. Even at that, most of them have doubtless crossed the Divide, and the balance of us soon will.

These intervening years have been busy ones, trying in my simple way to be useful to friends and neighbors. Perhaps I have not accomplished as much as some men do, yet I have used such talent as I have for the betterment of conditions about me. Just how long it will be before I'm called on to go on last relief I do not know; neither am I much concerned. I have on the whole tried to shoot a square life to such an extent that I can look any man in the face and tell him I have done him no wrong intentionally.

As time went on, the open range faded away as I had predicted in 1885, and what a pity it is that nature's great cow pasture should have been violated by sheep men and small farmers. Yet it seems that everything has its day, and in turn one dominating force gives way to another, and thus has it always been. The buffalo and Indian first dominated the country; then they passed, and the white man with his herds of domesticated animals took possession while he in turn gave way to an advancing civilization which has made a sorry mess of the country.

Long ago, the open range faded from the picture while nothing profitable has taken its place, and the condition is due to that greatest of civilizing factors, the railroad. One may, even today, ride in a Pullman from Crawford, Nebraska, to Sheridan, Wyoming, over a country where I had ridden for five summers, and he may observe from the car window the condition existing that I predicted in 1885.

As the train glides among the hills and over the prairie, one can see tumble-down shacks and perhaps a soddy or a dugout falling into decay as long ago the settler gave it up and returned to a country more suitable for continuing the battle for survival. The very sight of this country as it exists today would cause any old-time puncher to grab out his six-shooter and shoot everything to pieces as he visualizes the past.

Here in the big open spaces roamed herds of cattle so large that the likes of them are never seen now. Only the man who had a part in this great industry at the time can know the vastness of the large herds and of the wonderful bunch grass on which they lived and thrived. Now this wonderful grass has been destroyed by those root-eating sheep, which were such a sorry substitute for good, wholesome beef.

I look out of the car window, and as I recognize the same old country over which I had ridden as a young man, a great desire comes over me to mount to the hurricane deck of a cayuse and ride out among the hills in the thought that I might meet with a roundup and the same old gang of punchers with whom I associated so long, now almost a half century past.

The dream passes. I realize the impossibility of such dreams as I know that the large majority of those boys are on last relief and never again will be seen mounted on the hurricane deck of a cayuse chasing the festive bovines or riding a bucking bronc.

Now I am waiting to hear the call to go on last relief. Am I ready to part with home, loved ones, and pleasant surroundings? Fully realizing that my period of usefulness is about over, and my dependents are not dependent, I'll hustle around and make ready to answer Nature's last call, which will soon be given.

Appendix A

Letters from Friends

[Upon completion of one of the preliminary drafts of this manuscript, Reuben Mullins sent typewritten copies to old friends and colleagues from his cowboy days. These are among the letters he received in reply.]

Portales, New Mexico
7-12-'28

My dear Rube:

Almost a year ago I received your letter, and just through negligence I have failed to write, but was certainly glad to hear from you, and to learn that you have been so successful in life.

I—like you—often think of the AU7 ranch, and the boys who worked there. I am always glad to hear from any of them.

The only boys I have ever seen who worked with us there are Jim Williamson and Sam Mathers. Jim was out here to see me two years ago, his address is Leander, Texas. Sam's address was Kyle, Texas, when I saw him.

Since I have been here I have met two boys who used to work on the OS ranch, one's name was Bob Ferguson, the other Joe Bradley. I also met Mr. Hord—the 77 man at Fort Worth, Texas, at a cattle convention several years ago. Those are the only ones of the old boys I have seen since leaving the ranch.

Like you, I presume that Joe, and Hank Moore, and the older men who were there have passed over the "Divide."

I have not heard from Arch directly for thirty years. I sold some cattle to a man from Montana several years ago, and he told me that Arch went to Africa during the Boer war.

I heard that Sol Tuckerman went to Honolulu. Jimmie Tuff was running a Wild West Show the last time I knew of him.

Yes, I should like to have some of the roast ribs we used to have, also one of Fred's speckled pups, cooked in a flour sack, with the letters printed on it.

When the Indian uprising occurred in '90, Fred quit and joined the army as a scout.

You spoke of there being no "sore spot" toward me, nor any of the others,—there never was any with me. I may have seemed rough at times, but it was not from any personal feeling toward the men, just a matter of business.

I remember one time we rounded up near the corrals on Lodge Pole, just east of the ranch and you were riding a little, old blue pony that would not work to do any good, so I rode out to you and exchanged horses and the first cow I tried to cut out on him, he stopped on his front feet, his body went on, bowed up like a rainbow, so I decided at once that it was the horse instead of you that was at fault. I have often laughed about it since.

When I left Wyoming I went back to Texas and engaged in the cow business on my own hook, stayed there twelve years, and did very well, then sold out, and moved to New Mexico and was in the cow business here in a small way until three years ago, but I— like almost all cowmen in the southwest—became badly bent or broke when the deflation came after the war, and three years ago I suffered a nervous breakdown, and I sold my cattle, paid my debts, and have not done anything since.

I am glad you appreciate the Masonic order and have gone so high in the work. I am a member still.

My family consists of my wife—whom you knew—and two daughters. Ethel is a teacher. Ora is married; her husband is a newspaper man here.

If you have had your book published, please send me a copy and enclose the bill, and I'll remit the price. I shall enjoy reading it I am sure.

Please pardon this delay in answering and write me again. Your letters are always welcome. Tell me about any of the boys you know of.

With best wishes to yourself and family, I am,

Sincerely and fraternally yours,
J. B. Crawford

HARRY E. CRAIN

CHEYENNE, WYO.

November 24, 1931

Dear Mr. Mullins:

Your manuscript and letter was received some time ago, and I have read it very carefully and with a great deal of pleasure. The three years that you spent with us at the AU7 brings to my mind almost every instance that you speak of, and the only thing that bothers me at this time is, how in the world did you ever remember all that stuff.

I well remember the day you came home from the trip from the railroad, when you were caught out in the Cheyenne River bottom that winter night. You may remember that one of the first things you said to me when you reached the ranch was, "Thank God I had Harry Crain's big new coat on." You will remember that it was a new coat that Mr. Thomas had sent out to the ranch for me from Cheyenne.

You speak of Kirk Spaugh. You are mistaken there. His name was Curtis and we called him "Curt," and another slight error is, where you mentioned my name [you said] that I was born and raised in Boston. This is in error. I was born and raised in Vermont, but went to Boston for two years and Mr. Thomas brought me to Cheyenne to go to the AU7 ranch. Also you speak of Jimmy Tuff. Now, Jimmie Tuff has been living for a good many years in Omaha. This last summer he was retired and a young man from Cheyenne has taken his place with some painting company. I do not know if Jimmy is still living there or if he went back to New York City where his parents all live. One other incident that might have slipped your mind. The time we were on the beef roundup down on the Cheyenne River when it was so cold and stormy. Mr. Thomas was along with us, and do you remember the man who was with him? He was Mr. Ames, one of the principal owners of the outfit, and one of the noted Ames family of Boston.

I am sending you a little booklet which will explain itself. I trust you will see a good many names in this that you are familiar with. I could have sent this book to you sooner, but I have been expecting Senator John B. Kendrick here in Cheyenne for the past week. I only learned yesterday that he does not plan to come this way on his trip to Washington. I would have liked to have had him read it. I know he would have been pleased very much as he always is interested in that kind of stuff, although he is a very busy man he never misses an opportunity to look out for some of the old stuff of the early life on the range.

However, I did take the liberty of letting Mr. Logan read this manuscript. You may remember Mr. Logan as the man who made the Logan bits for the cow punchers in the early days.

I surely wish you abundant success in disposing of this book, and I want to be one of the first ones to purchase a copy.

With kindest personal regards, I am

Very sincerely yours,
Harry E. Crain

Wheatland, Wyoming
October 25, 1931

Dear Mr. Mullins:

You have, no doubt, wondered why my father has not written you about the manuscript that you sent him to read. As he can't write himself, it is of course hard for him to get an answer written as soon as he would like.

We enjoyed reading the book very much and thought you were quite true in your description of the early days in Wyoming. The rest of us in the family read and were quite amused at your characterization of Daddy. And we had to tease him a little about being so "hard-boiled." He said that he remembered and had known many of the men you wrote about. He feels that if he could talk to you about these days you two would have many interesting things to review. It is hard to write them to you.

I know that he is very thankful to you for being so kind to send him your book and he enjoyed going back to the old days with you in the story. The rest of us are grateful to you also. We hope that you will be successful in your publication of your manuscript.

Most Sincerely,
Dorothy J. Grant

City of Omaha

Executive Office
James C. Dahlman, Mayor

September 21, 1927

My dear Doctor Mullins:

For the past several days, I have been enjoying a perusal of your manuscript, and I want to congratulate you upon your faithful portrayal of your activities of the early days. I was delighted with your description of the roundups, the branding, the hay-making, and the numerous little anecdotes that intersperse the vivid pictures of cowboy life of the early eighties. Your memory is positively photographic and one has no trouble visualizing the circumstances about which you write.

I hope every reader of this interesting work will find in it the pleasure it has given me.

With kind personal regards and good wishes, I am,

Sincerely yours,
James C. Dahlman
Mayor

The First National Bank

Col. Chas. F. Coffee, President
Chadron, Nebr.

May 9, 1934

Dear Mr. Mullins:

Yesterday I expressed back to you the manuscript that you had been good enough to send my father to read. He enjoyed it very much and it brought back to his memory many old friends and events.

I want to apologize for the looks of the manuscript, but my father is hard on whatever he is reading and could not help mussing it up.

Thank you very much for sending it up, I am

Yours very truly,
C.F. Coffee, Jr.

Appendix B

About the Author

The five years that Reuben Baker Mullins spent as a cowboy in Wyoming were indeed exciting ones. But most of Mullins' life was lived with this same gusto, as can be seen by the accounts recorded in several documents, one of the most remarkable of which is an autobiography detailing his family history as well as his own experiences from childhood until three years before his death.

Born in Missouri in 1863, Reuben was the third of William and Anna Mullins' six children. Most of his childhood, however, was spent in Blakesburg, Iowa.

Working hard to survive was always a part of the Mullins family creed, and Reuben did more than his share. By the time he was nine years old, Reuben was doing farm chores, working the long hours of an adult. He recalls working a week of twelve-hour days for one farmer and receiving a silver dollar for his week's labor. Elated with this amount of money, he rushed home to share it with his mother, a habit he kept until she died.

In addition to working at a number of enterprises, which included a futile attempt at tobacco farming where he taught himself to smoke in order to consume the unsold portion of his crop, Reuben completed six grades of school. He was, by his own admission, not a good student, however. Although he sensed the importance of education, he just could not seem to learn at the rate the other students did and hence quit when he was fourteen, not to return to school until he was thirty-two. Eventually, he went on to complete both a medical and a dental degree.

At the age of fifteen, without any money and without saying good-bye to his family, Reuben left home, going "down the dusty road with his face to the West."

Reuben's initial foray into the adult work world was at Red Cloud, Nebraska, where he was hired by a farmer to do chores for room and board. Before too many weeks had passed, his clothes and shoes were full of holes. With no prospects of replacing them,

Reuben wrapped his thin blanket around his shoulders and set out on a cold, November morning to return to Coal Field, Iowa, to seek work as a miner. After traveling several hundred miles by foot and by rail, he arrived in Albia, just a few miles from his home. However, he did not even consider returning to live with his family since he felt that they had enough mouths to feed without him. Besides, he did not want to risk being known as a "quitter." Instead, he hiked through the night the remaining nine miles to his friend's house where, half-starved and shivering violently from the early morning cold, he was taken in, fed, and given a job as a miner's "buddy" to this friend. Thus began the first of several trades that Reuben was to learn during the course of his long life.

Reuben was goaded by the drive to learn a trade, to make a living. His first career as a coal miner was a trade he relied on for many years, even during those while he cowboyed, to provide employment during the winter months when cowboys could not work on the snowy Wyoming plains. He supplemented that trade with another he learned while working in the Iowa coal mines. In Coal Field he became acquainted with a blacksmith named Hart by helping out with the bellows; Mr. Hart consequently asked him if he wanted to learn blacksmithing. Reuben quickly accepted and soon found this a fine arena for his strong, natural abilities in mechanics.

During the next few years, Reuben continued to perfect his blacksmithing skills, working in mines at Coal Field, Knoxville Junction, and Centerville. In Centerville, under the tutelage of Sandy Dargavle, Reuben picked up the Scots brogue which later aided him in getting his first job in Wyoming. It was also while he was working at Centerville that he learned the boxing skills which he used to knock out the Indian athlete, Al, during his time with the AU7 Ranch. A small-framed man, Reuben had always wanted to learn to protect himself, so when offered the opportunity to learn to box with the Scots miners when they entertained themselves during their lunch hour, he leaped at it. He stuck with the sport even though his face became so sore he could not shave, until finally his Scots instructors declared he had grown so clever with the gloves that he was able to take care of himself.

In April, 1883, Reuben returned to mining, but when work slowed he was laid off. He then decided to head for Rock Springs, Wyoming, to get a job in the mines a thousand miles further west. Leaving his gear packed in a trunk with the family he had been living with, he set off in search of his future.

When the train stopped in Cheyenne, Reuben liked the country so much that he decided to stay there instead of going on to Rock Springs. He quickly found work as a blacksmith. His first job, on the construction of the Sybille Ditch some eighty miles north of Cheyenne, was short-lived as he became disheartened when his bunk buddy was summarily hung after a drunken shooting incident. Hiking the eighty miles back to Cheyenne, Reuben looked for another job and soon was hired by the Swan Land and Cattle Company as a blacksmith at their shop in Chugwater. There he gained considerable experience shoeing stage horses while also earning the respect of both the freighters and the cowboys who brought their horses to be shod. During his summer's work, he not only learned the lore of cowboying but was allowed to participate in a roundup after surviving his first greenhorn prank. By the time the shop closed for the winter, Reuben was determined to return the next year, only this time as a cowboy rather than as a blacksmith. And so he did, for he spent the next six summers and one winter cowboying on the Wyoming range.

Those times that Reuben was not cowboying he spent working either in the mines or as a blacksmith. Most of the time he went back to Iowa to work in the mines there, but he also found work at times in the mines being opened in Wyoming. In the winter of 1885–86 he opened his own blacksmith shop in Douglas, Wyoming, but the town itself was too new to support his shop. Failing in this enterprise, still in his cowboy clothes he applied for a job at a mine near Shawnee. Not only the owner of the mine but the other miners as well were suspicious of Reuben's capabilities, for they had seen other cowboys fail miserably in such work. Reuben, however, surprised them, for in only one day he had made such progress that they knew a skilled miner was at work.

During this winter Reuben met his first wife, Elizabeth Kirby, at the Kirby boarding house where he was staying, though he did not marry her until the winter of 1887–88. In the meantime he spent the summer of 1886 cowboying for the AU7 Ranch, the intervening winter at the What Cheer mine in Iowa, and the summer of 1887 again cowboying, first at the 4W Ranch under Billy Keating, foreman, and then at the Hoe Ranch under Frank Laberteaux.

When winter came again, Reuben found employment as a blacksmith for a granger not too far from the Hoe spread. Not being able to tolerate either the living conditions there or the disposition of his employer, he quit after a short time, moving on to Glenrock, near Douglas, where a new mine had recently opened. After starting to work there, Reuben was able to marry Elizabeth.

With the spring of 1888 came a slowing down of work in the Glenrock mine, so Reuben returned to the range for his last summer as a cowboy, again riding for the Hoe Ranch. Though he had realized his dream of cowboying for what he considered the most desirable outfit around, riding the best string of horses and working for one of the best foremen in any outfit, Reuben began to lose interest in this way of life. He felt that the future of the cattle business, if it followed the old patterns of the open range, was doomed both by the advent of the railroad and by an influx of settlers who were fencing off water from range stock. Further, as a married man, he saw little future in a life that was limited to thirty-five or forty dollars a month for seasonal work. So at the end of the fall roundup after the cattle were loaded for shipment at Chadron, Reuben quit range life forever, selling off all his gear, including his Visalia saddle, as a note of finality. Saying his farewells, he returned to Glenrock and his pregnant wife.

Back in Glenrock, Reuben found a job and a home for his growing family. Here Elizabeth and Reuben's son, Richard, was born in 1889. Though life for them initially looked bright, circumstances soon forced first a separation and then a divorce.

Because work in the Glenrock mine quit altogether, Reuben returned to Iowa to work in mines there. After short stays in What Cheer and Centerville, Reuben landed a job as a mine blacksmith in Mendota, Missouri. As prearranged, Reuben sent for his family to join him, only to receive a letter in return telling him that the Glenrock mine had reopened and the blacksmith job there was his. Reluctantly he returned, as he wanted his family to be together.

Unfortunately this effort ultimately did not pay off. Mining activity again slowed in Glenrock. Hearing of a new mine opening at Cambria some hundred and fifty miles northeast of Glenrock, which was supposed to employ a large force of men steadily all year, Reuben and Elizabeth decided he should try for work there.

After only two weeks, Reuben was asked to take charge of one of the Cambria mine's three blacksmith shops, and he headed the shop until he left the Cambria mines two years later. Sending for his family to join him, Reuben found that his wife did not wish to leave her family in Glenrock. Despite his pleas, the situation did not alter, and so after about a year Reuben took steps to divorce her.

For a social life Reuben turned to fraternal organizations. He helped start an I.O.O.F. Lodge in Newcastle and a Knights of Pythias Lodge in Cambria; then he requested in 1892 to take the Blue Lodge degrees in the Free Masons, continuing up through all thirty-two degrees until he received the thirty-third honorary degree in 1917.

During this period he met Dr. Verbryck, the mine doctor and a fellow Mason, who indirectly created the confidence in Reuben to strive for better things than remaining connected with coal mining. Before taking those steps, however, Reuben spent the next year in charge of a blacksmith shop at a mine in Chandler, Colorado.

While he was at Chandler, Reuben received a letter from his brother Charles, who had been practicing medicine in Eagle, Nebraska, since graduating from medical school two years earlier. Charles proposed to open a drugstore in Eagle and wanted Reuben to join him as a partner. At first Reuben scoffed at the idea that he—in his words "just a tramp mine blacksmith, coal miner, cowboy, and what have you"—could possibly make a go of it as a druggist. Then, remembering Dr. Verbryck and how he did not really seem any more intelligent on many matters than Reuben felt himself to be, Reuben decided to give the enterprise a try. Shortly thereafter he found himself in Eagle in charge of clerking at the store. In his spare time he studied the first principles of chemistry, physiology, and *Materia-Medica*, finding that the more he studied these subjects, the more he liked them. Unfortunately, he did not have long to study, for their business, though it initially thrived, failed after two months because of the Cleveland Panic of 1893.

With no money, since he had invested all of his in this venture, Reuben returned to Cambria and his former job as blacksmith at one of the mines. But he took with him some of these medical books and a desire to learn more. During the day he continued as a blacksmith, but now he saved every penny he earned, investing in more books which he pored over every night in his room. Since he had not been in school for over fifteen years, he had difficulty concentrating, but with the encouragement of friends, he managed to overcome his lack of formal education and prepare for medical school. In August of 1895 at the age of thirty-two Reuben quit his job, turned his back on the friends and the work which had sustained him for so long, and looked ahead to an entirely new career in medicine. He had saved five hundred dollars, which he calculated would carry him through two years of medical school. The rest he would worry about as he went along. His immediate hurdle was passing the entrance examinations.

Reuben spent the next three years attending the Medical College at Omaha, Nebraska. Of his class of forty-one, thirty-six males and five females, Reuben was probably the most mature, enthusiastic, and hard-working. He rapidly progressed through the course of study. His first summer vacation was spent in the free clinics the medical school ran and in which medical students were exposed to a variety of on-the-spot diagnoses which improved their skills. His second summer vacation gave him even more practice in diagnosing as he spent this time serving the small community of Oconto some twenty-five miles from Broken Bow as its sole doctor. Assessing the value of this experience later, Reuben felt that he had had better luck with those patients than he did with later ones. He notes, "After checking up on my patients at the end of my vacation, I found I had not lost one even though I had several difficult cases which persisted in getting well despit [sic] all I did."

At the close of his summer's work when he had paid all his expenses, Reuben found that he was three hundred dollars to the good, enough, he felt, to carry him through his last year of medical school. So he returned to Omaha for the third time, where he was selected to work as a special assistant to the skilled surgeon, Dr. Jonas, who was shortly thereafter appointed Surgeon General for the Union Pacific Railroad. In the spring of 1898, Reuben and twenty-six other members of his class passed their examinations, becoming fully certified M.D.'s. Reuben noted with satisfaction that he had accomplished in three years what he had initially thought would take him five.

Out of medical school, Reuben moved to Broken Bow to cover his brother Charles's practice and care for Charles's family while Charles himself went off to serve as a surgeon to the First Nebraska Regiment during the Spanish American War. When Charles returned the following March, Reuben moved to Sargent, some forty miles away, and established his own practice. As it flourished, Reuben settled into the community, marrying Mamie Snyder, a teacher he had met while practicing in Oconto the previous summer. However, Reuben was not satisfied with the country around Sargent and moved instead to Gering, a small community in the extreme western part of Nebraska. He was immediately successful, doing thirty dollars' worth of business the first two days he was there and so much thereafter that he was hard pressed to keep up with the demand.

His second day in Gering Reuben was approached by a small, red-haired man who turned out to be Billy Keating, former foreman of the 4W Ranch. Keating, his wife, and four children had relocated in Gering, where Billy ran a small bunch of cattle in the nearby hills. Deciding Gering would be a good place for them to live, too, Reuben sent for his wife, and they lived with the Keatings until they were able to find a place of their own.

For the next three years, Reuben practiced medicine successfully. However, he became increasingly discontent with its demands on his time, especially since he was frequently called upon to drive long distances over bumpy roads, a condition which eventually created inflammation of his sciatic nerve and an inability to walk or ride comfortably. In addition he and his wife, Mamie, could never do anything social, even attend church, since Reuben was always on call. So Reuben decided a change of career was in order. The most logical choice, it seemed to him, was dentistry, which was closely related to the field of medicine so that he was already familiar with much of the necessary background. Further positive aspects were that dentistry required a large amount of mechanical work, which had always appealed to Reuben, and it would not require his being called from a warm bed on a cold night to attend a patient. Over the objections of his wife's family, Reuben prepared to spend two more years in college in order to earn another medical degree.

In June of 1901 Reuben retired from practicing medicine and moved back to Broken Bow, where he and his wife built a small cottage as their permanent home. October found them ensconced in an apartment in Omaha as Reuben prepared to begin coursework. Because of his previous degree, he was advanced to junior status and progressed rapidly through the courses, largely because of his natural mechanical abilities. To supplement his savings and help cover their expenses, Reuben turned to bushwacking, a time-honored though illegal practice of treating, without supervision, patients in one's home for a small fee. Though not sanctioned by either faculty or practicing dentists, still the practice continued, providing for many the only means for them to continue school.

Reuben successfully passed the examinations held at the end of his junior year and earned a certificate in dentistry. This certificate made him eligible for a state license and the status of legal practitioner, though he had yet to complete a final year of coursework to earn the actual degree. He and Mamie then returned to Broken Bow where Reuben soon was making even more money than he had made as a doctor. He remained there until the fall of 1904 when he moved to Baltimore to finish his final year at the University of Maryland, a move which would qualify him for a degree in dentistry.

Reuben and Mamie found living quarters near the university and Reuben applied himself to his coursework. He progressed until the spring of 1905 when tragedy struck. As Reuben left his lecture room at ten o'clock the last Monday in February, a man met him with word that his wife was seriously ill. She was operated on at eleven o'clock for complications resulting from a tubal pregnancy. This first operation proved unsuccessful as did a second one performed later, and she died on Thursday from peritonitis. Devastated, Reuben accompanied her body back to Broken Bow where the funeral was held.

When he returned to Baltimore, Reuben plunged immediately back into classes. However, he was unable to concentrate and so spent much time that spring touring the east coast, sightseeing. Though he did not take his final examinations, when the results were in, he discovered he had still passed and hence had earned a degree in dentistry to go with his degree in medicine.

Upon returning to Broken Bow, Reuben found himself again in possession of a busy practice which, however, did little to alleviate his sense of loneliness. He turned once again to the fraternalism of lodge work. But even though his lodge work and a busy practice helped occupy his mind, Reuben missed having a home. About this time he met Edna Konkel, who had come to him for some dental work. Though she was some twenty years his junior, they were married shortly thereafter in May, 1906, and lived happily until Reuben died in 1935 at the age of seventy-two.

During this marriage, Reuben and Edna had two sons: Gifford, born 1909, died 1983; and Robert, born 1911, died 1984. Gifford in turn had two children, Ronald Bruce, who was born in 1940 and presently resides in Lincoln, Nebraska; and Priscilla Ann, who was born in 1944 and is now married to Avery Rexford Hogan of St. Louis, Missouri. Robert had no children. Reuben's eldest son, Richard, by Elizabeth Kirby, had three children: Richard, born 1914, died 1915; Kathryn Elizabeth, born 1915, died 1987; and Helen Bernice, born 1917, still living.

Reuben continued to practice as a dentist throughout the remainder of his life. At age fifty-six Reuben decided to move his family to Fremont where he felt his two sons would be able to attend good schools in a wholesome environment. Reuben practiced in Fremont until he retired.

Reuben had always enjoyed traveling, and he and Edna did so extensively throughout their life together. In 1912 he made a trip to Sheridan, Wyoming, stopping off in Cambria on the return trip to visit his old friends at the mine there. Later trips with his wife and sons allowed Reuben to meet once again old friends from his cowboy days and introduce them to his family. One of these trips was an automobile trip to Cheyenne to attend the rodeo. At the same time, Reuben looked up Harry Crain, whom he had not seen since 1888 when Harry was still wrangling horses at the AU7 Ranch. Now Crain was a prominent banker in Cheyenne and was delighted to sit and reminisce with Reuben over their cowboy days. Crain was able to tell Reuben of the whereabouts of many of their crew, including their old foreman, Jim Crawford, who was in the cattle business in Portales, New Mexico. On this same trip Reuben returned to Glenrock to visit his son Richard and his family, his first to that town in more than thirty-two years though he and Richard had exchanged visits more frequently than that. Throughout this trip Reuben was appalled at the damaging effect human habitation had wrought on the open range he remembered from his cowboy days and noted how often changes are not necessarily good.

Reuben was certainly in a position to make that assessment, for in the course of his long, active life he saw many changes and technological advances, the Great War, a stock market boom and bust, and the beginnings of the Depression. He saw the country through good times and bad, under politicians he approved of and others whom he scorned. Yet through it all, he clung to the philosophy which guided everything he undertook. As he himself notes, "From the first, mine was a veritable school of hard knocks, and the most valuable lesson I learned very early in life was to depend on my own efforts and judgment, which is so necessary in every successful life."

After he was sixty years of age, Reuben began writing and produced the manuscript contained here as well as several others. He recounts that he worked steadily at his typewriter when not busy at other work even before he retired from dentistry because he was convinced that one should remain productive. Writing articles that covered a range of topics from "The Cowboy Doctor" to "Dental Prophylaxis in World Schools," Reuben continued to record his experiences and impressions until he died in 1935 of a cerebral hemorrhage. He was seventy-two.

Reuben Baker Mullins lived an interesting life with dogged determination. Of that fact no doubt exists. What makes him different from others with similar experiences are the amazingly accurate and intriguing accounts he left of this life. He was indeed one of that stalwart breed who helped settle the West, and he contributed both to the frontier experience as well as to the civilizing experience. He saw the frontier of the 1860s turn into the mechanical age of the 1930s, which meant he saw the advent of such inventions as the telephone, the incandescent lamp, photography, and the widespread use of electricity. He saw the boom and bust of the economy several times, but his indomitable spirit served him well and his call for "last relief" was answered willingly.

Further Reading

Cattle Brands Owned by Members of the Wyoming Stock Growers Association. Chicago: J. W. Jones Stationery & Printing, 1882.

Clawson, Marion. *The Western Range Livestock Industry.* New York: McGraw-Hill, 1950.

Clay, John. *My Life on the Range.* Chicago: Privately Printed, 1924.

Crain, Harry, comp. *Letters From Old Friends and Members of the Wyoming Stock Growers Association.* Cheyenne: S.A. Bristol, 1923.

Frink, Maurice. *Cow Country Cavalcade: Eighty Years of the Wyoming Stock Growers Association.* Denver: Old West Publishing, 1954.

Frink, Maurice, Turrentine Jackson, and Agnes Wright Spring. *When Grass was King.* Boulder: University of Colorado Press, 1956.

Gress, Kathryn. *Ninety Years Cow Country: A Factual History of the Wyoming Stock Growers Association.* NP.: Wyoming Stock Growers Association, 1963.

Heidt, William, Jr., ed. *Addie Smiley's Letters from the West: 1882–1886.* Ithaca, New York: De Witt Historical Society, 1955.

Historical Committee of the Robbers Roost Historical Society, comp. *Pioneering on the Cheyenne River: The Stories of Pioneers and Early Settlers in Northern Niobrara County, Wyoming; Southern Weston County, Wyoming; Western Fall River County, South Dakota.* 1947. reprint. Lusk, Wyoming: The Lusk Herald, 1956.

Larson, T.A. *History of Wyoming,* 2d ed., rev. Lincoln: University of Nebraska Press, 1978.

Morris, Robert C. *Collections of the Wyoming Historical Society.* Cheyenne: The Wyoming Historical Society, 1897.

Mothershead, Harmon Ross. *Swan Land and Cattle Company, Ltd.* Norman: University of Oklahoma Press, 1971.

Nimmo, Joseph. *Report in Regard to the Range and Ranch Cattle Business of the United States.* Washington, D.C.: U.S. Printing Office, 1885.

Osgood, Ernest Staples. *The Day of the Cattleman.* 1929. reprint. Chicago: University of Chicago Press, 1957.

Pelzer, Louis. *The Cattleman's Frontier.* Glendale, California: Arthur H. Clark, 1936.

Spring, Agnes Wright. *Seventy Years.* Gillette, Wyoming: Wyoming Stock Growers Association, 1942.

Strahorn, Robert E. *Handbook of Wyoming and Guide to the Black Hills and Big Horn Regions.* Cheyenne: [Chicago: Knight & Leonard], 1877.

Triggs, J. H. *History of Cheyenne and Northern Wyoming, Embracing the Gold Fields of the Black Hills, Powder River, and Big Horn Countries.* Omaha, Nebraska: Herald Steam Book and Job Printing House, 1876.

Urbanek, Mae. *Wyoming Place Names.* Boulder, Colo.: Johnson Publishing, 1974.

Wyoming: A Guide to Its History, Highways, and People. 1941. reprint. Introduction by T. A. Larson. Lincoln: University of Nebraska Press, 1981.

Index

Al (half-breed Indian), 30, 36–37;
    footrace 55–58, 115
Albia, Iowa, 153, 204
Aliases (for cowboys), 64
Alkali water, 93
Ames, Mr., 104, 199
Antelope, 34, 88, 145, 147
Arizona, 56
Arkansas, 109, 112, 113
AU7 Ranch, 26–27, 38, 55, 63,
    64, 104, 109, 112, 118, 132, 136,
    147, 150, 154, 155, 156, 163,
    173, 178, 197, 199

Banjo, 110
Bar T Ranch, 115
Bed, preparation of, 31; care of,
    52, 54
Belle Fourche, 44
Belle Fourche Creek, 169
Big Horn Mountains, 167, 175
Black, Frank, 112–113
Black Hills, 44
Black Hills Trail, 13
Blacklisting cowboys, 78
Blacksmithing, 3, 4, 11, 12, 13;
    buying supplies for AU7, 28–
    29; setting up shop at AU7, 40–
    41, 42, 84–85, 130, 132, 133,
    137, 149, 171, 172, 180, 187,
    188, 204–207
Blair, Henry (owner of Hoe
    Ranch), 13, 182–183, 186, 190
Blue (fiddle player), 110
Boer War, 197

Bolin, Jack, 162, 163, 172, 184,
    191
Boston, Massachusetts, 63, 97,
    100, 104, 199
Bowie, Al (Swan Land and Cattle
    Company General Manger), 12,
    15
Boxing, 30, 36, 37, 110, 128, 204
Bradburg, Mr. (contractor on
    Sybille Ditch), 4
Bradley, Joe, 197
Branding pens, 43, 91, 128
Breaking broncs, 138–140
Bridle Bit Ranch, 55, 58, 100
Buffalo (American bison), 44, 194
Building cabin on AU7, 122–123
Burlington Railroad depot, 25

Calamity Jane, 134
California, 32
Cards, 36, 40
Carey, Joseph M. Jr. (former
    governor), 13, 99
Carlyle (University), 91
Carter, Nick, 111
"Carve" cattle, 22, 165, 177
Cattle: herd described, 66–68, 74;
    night herding, 70; paraded for
    foreign visitors to elicit capital,
    81; roundups, 53, 65–68, 91,
    96–97; working cattle, 91; day
    herd, 72, 73, 97; shipping, 97–
    100; night herd, 97; danger of
    stampede, 95
Chadron, Nebraska, 13, 97, 99,

Chadron *(cont.)*
100, 101, 102, 124, 129, 149, 183, 184, 191
Charcoal, for blacksmith work on AU7, 42
Checkers, 36, 40, 111
Cheyenne-Deadwood Stage, 14
Cheyenne River, 26, 27, 28, 35, 75, 98, 112, 116, 154, 155, 199
Cheyenne, Wyoming, 1, 7, 8, 9, 10, 11, 12, 23, 26, 27, 30, 43, 80, 85, 99, 112, 126
Chicago, Illinois, 23, 24, 81, 97, 100, 149, 182, 183
Chugwater, Wyoming, 10, 11, 12, 14, 27, 30, 31, 165
Chugwater Ranch, 13
Cleveland, Grover, 25
Clothing, 1, 29, 39, 43, 83, 181
Coal, 28, 41, 42, 134, 171, 178, 187
Coffee, Charley F. (owner of an outfit in Hat Creek Basin and banker in Chadron, Nebraska), 13, 202
Colt pistol, 43, 117
Cooking/eating, 1, 5, 6, 18, 25, 30, 31, 36, 38, 41, 42, 47, 61, 68, 69, 70, 75, 83, 87, 89, 90, 91, 96, 101, 102, 103, 105, 106, 114, 115, 117, 123–124, 125, 151, 154, 155, 157, 162, 175, 176, 182, 183, 184, 186, 188, 195
Cooties, 5
Cowboys, appearance of, 1–2, 26; view of, 64, 98–99
Coyotes, 9
Crain, Harry, 51, 61, 63, 69, 75, 99, 100, 106, 108, 111, 114, 135, 210
Crawford, Arch, 43, 51, 72, 114, 115, 126, 138, 197
Crawford, Ethel, 110, 198
Crawford, James B. (Jim), 27, 28, 29, 35, 40, 41, 42, 51, 56, 57,

64, 65, 68, 69, 73, 74, 79, 84, 93, 96, 97, 98, 99, 103, 106, 109, 110, 112, 118, 122, 125, 127, 130, 131, 132, 135, 137, 138, 146, 148, 155, 197–198, 211
Crawford, Nebraska, 194
Crawford, Ora, 198
Cribbage, 111

Dahlman, James C., 102, 201
Day herding, 72–73
Deer, 88
Democrats, Kentucky, 25
Des Moines, Iowa, 150
Desmonds, 1, 2
Devils Tower, 44, 46
Dominoes, 111
Douglas, Wyoming, 101, 129, 132, 133, 134, 136, 183, 189, 205
Drunks, 6, 26, 35
Duffy, Tom, 12

Eating/cooking, 1, 5, 6, 18, 25, 30, 31, 36, 38, 41, 42, 47, 61, 68, 69, 70, 75, 83, 87, 89, 90, 91, 96, 101, 102, 103, 105, 106, 114, 115, 117, 123–124, 125, 151, 154, 155, 157, 162, 175, 176, 182, 183, 184, 186, 188, 195
Edgemont, South Dakota, 98
English and Scottish money in ranching, 80–82

Fallen Leaf (Indian woman), 32
Ferguson, Bob, 197
Fiddle, 110
Fiddleback Ranch, 13, 17, 157
Fire on prairie, 184–186
Fort Laramie, 32
Fort Worth, Texas, 197
4W Ranch, 13, 123, 124, 154, 156, 160, 161, 162, 205, 208
Fred (cook on AU7), 38, 54, 58, 75, 76, 94, 101, 106, 119, 135, 136, 139, 198

Frontier Days in Cheyenne, 63

Gambling, 10–11, 26, 33, 56, 101, 134; with Indians, 88, 89
Glenrock, Wyoming, 189
Gold Room (saloon), 10, 27, 56
Grant, Dorothy, 200–201
Grant, Duncan, 15, 16, 18, 19, 20, 21, 22, 23, 29, 200–201
Great Spirit, 57
Greeley, Horace, 1
Groves, Sam, 13, 157

Haircuts, 156–158
Hat Creek Basin, 13, 34
Hat Creek Store, 35, 111, 136, 148, 154
Hay, 84–86
Heart and Hand, 111
Hereford bulls, 80
Hilderbrand, Charles, 179
Hord, T.B., 13, 197
Hoe Ranch, 13, 161, 162, 178, 181, 186, 189, 192
Horse Creek, 179
Horse herd, described, 50; parceled out, 51–52, 129
House of David, 157
Hunter, Colin, 13
Hynds, Harry, 30

Indians, mount horse on right side, 19, 88; white man flayed alive for killing one, 32; food, 86, 87; braves do not work, 88; gambling, 89; pinto horses, preferred by Indian, 88; squaws' roles, 89; tanning hides by Indians, 89; basic needs, 89, 125–126; Indian burial ground, 178
Iowa, 150, 203, 204
Irwin [Irvine?], Billy, 13

James, Jesse, 111
Jerry (young friend of Mullins), 6, kills cook, 7, is hanged, 8

Kangaroo Court, 109–110, 113, 120
Keating, Billy, 13, 123, 124, 156, 158, 160, 162, 205, 208
Kelly, Hiram B., 13
Kendrick, John B., 13, 99, 160, 200
Kentucky, 124
King Solomon's Temple, 123
Knoxville, Iowa, 150
Kyle, Texas, 197

Laberteaux, Frank, 161, 162, 164, 165, 166, 171, 172, 175, 177, 180, 183, 184, 186, 187, 191, 192
Lance Creek, 35, 36, 55, 65, 66, 148, 179
Lathrop, George, 12
Letter writing to females, 111–113
Little Thunder Creek, 93
Locoed horse, 51–52
Lodge Pole Creek, 27, 43, 45, 47, 74, 75, 198
Logan, Mr., 200
Luck, Hard, 13
Lusk, Frank, 13, 17, 34
Lusk, Wyoming, 13, 17, 34, 136, 148, 154
LX Ranch, 179

McCluskey, 3
Mathers, Sam, 25, 26, 27, 28, 29, 30, 31, 36, 37, 39, 40, 41, 43, 45, 48, 49, 56, 57, 59, 61, 63, 84, 86–87, 101, 122, 123, 138, 197
Marriage, James Crawford, 122
Masonic Order, 198, 206–207
Mavericks and mavericking, 77–79
Montana, 180, 197
Moore, Hank, 114, 197
Moore, Lee, 13
Mosquitoes, 84
Mowing machine, 80, 84–85, 171
Mule Creek, 147
Mullins, R.B., goes West, 1;

Mullins, R.B. *(cont.)*
blacksmithing, 3; turns twenty-one, 3; hired at Sybille Ditch, 3, leaves for Cheyenne, 8; decides to be a cowboy, 11; goes to work for Swan Land and Cattle Company, 11; first day cowboying, 18–23; rides bucking horse, 19–20; votes for first time, 25; goes to work for AU7, buys blacksmith equipment, 28; buys cowboy outfit, 29; boxing experience, 30; travels to ranch, 30–38; fight with Al, 37; sets up blacksmith shop, 40; goes on ride to see countryside, 44; works town herd, 47–50; general roundup, 53; slow race, 59–61; roundup, 63; rides Blue, 63; night guard, 71; singing, 70; day herd, 68–73; trailing cattle, 74; rustlers, 77; black ball of cowboys by association, 77; mavericking, 77–79; makes running irons, 78–79; repairs mowing machine, 84; sees Indian, 86; views on mistreatment of Indians, 90; working calves, 91–92; finds spring, 93; roundup, 94; handling beef herd, 94; trail drive, 97; view of cowboys, 98; recalls Theodore Roosevelt, 99; complains of poor images of cowboys, 99; helps gather herd, 100; rides night herd, 105; endures cold weather, 105–106, roundup ends, 107; men paid off, 109; love letters, 111; lost in blizzard, 116–118; worst storm in history, 120–122; sees dead cattle, 121; Sioux Indian "raid," 125–126; sees ranchers retrench on hiring, 129; starts a new year, 129; poor year following storm, 130; predicts end of cattle business, 131; leaves AU7,
132; sets up shop in Douglas, 133; goes broke and leaves Douglas, 133; goes to work in mine in Shawnee, Wyoming, 134, 135; helps break Oregon broncs, 137; breaks Shawnee (horse), 139–140; rides Shawnee, 141–143; George pitches off in thorns, 144; rides to Lusk and back, 148; gets lost in prairie, 149; takes last order from Jim, 150; leaves AU7, 150; goes to Des Moines, 150; meets female mail correspondent, 152; goes to Albia, Iowa, 153; goes back to Wyoming, 154; passes by AU7, 154; goes to 4W, 156; cuts hair, 157; is thrown by falling horse, 159; becomes a rep, 160; goes to work for Hoe Ranch, 161; roundup on Hoe, 163; builds fire protector, 172; fixes tools on 21 Ranch, 174; burning coal mine, 178; roundup on 21 Ranch, 182; trades saddle, 179; swims river, 181; fights range fire, 185–186; leaves Hoe Ranch, 186; goes to granger ranch, 187; hurts back, 188; leaves granger ranch, 189; sells outfit, 192
Mullins, Miss (Keating), 123–124
Music, 36, 40, 110

National Museum, Washington, D.C., 179
New Mexico, 198
New York, 199
Nicholas, Mr., (ran a sub-camp for Sybille Ditch Project), 4, 6
Nicknames, 64
Night horses, 71
9 9 9 Ranch, 55, 56, 114, 116, 117, 118, 147, 148
Northwestern Railroad, 99, 101, 103, 114, 128–129, 132, 149, 184

Oil, 176
Old Woman Creek, 148
Oelrichs, South Dakota, 115
Omaha, Nebraska, 25, 102, 199, 201
Oregon broncs, 136–140
OS Ranch, 13, 55, 56, 58, 65, 74, 76, 86, 92, 103, 155, 173, 197
Ottumea, Iowa, 25
Overstock ranges in 1885, 73
OW Ranch, 13, 160, 161

Penney, Fred, 127–128
Pistols, 1, 7, 57, 102, 110, 117, 134, 157, 177; firing of to control livestock, 60, 68
Platte River, 129, 132
Powder River, 62, 161, 166, 167, 169, 178, 179, 180, 184, 192
Prairie dogs, 20
Prairie fire, 184–185
Pumpkin Buttes, 166, 184

Range overstocked in 1885, 73
Rattlesnakes, 177
Rawhide Creek, 32, 34
Rep (representative), 53–54, 55, 69, 86, 160
Repairing mowing machine, 84, 171
Revere, Paul, 155
Richards, DeForest, 13
Riding night herd, 105
Rocky Mountains, 169
Roosevelt, Theodore, 99
Ross, Nellie, 99, 100
Roundup (largest in Wyoming), 53
Running iron (described), 78
Running Water Creek, 34, 160

Sahara Desert, 159
Salt Creek, 175, 176, 177
Sand Creek, 5, 8
Scotchman, 11, 15, 204

Scottish and English money in ranching, 80–81
77 Ranch, 197
76 Ranch, 13
Shakespeare, William, 111
Shawnee, Wyoming, 134, 136
Sheep come to Wyoming ranges, 190
Sheridan, Phil, 155
Sheridan, Wyoming, 52, 194, 210
Sherman, General William Tecumseh, 144
Sidney Stage Crossing, 160
Simmonds Hotel, 26
Singing, 70, 97, 98
Sioux Indians, 86, 125
Slickers, 67, 106, 157
Slow Race, 59–61
Snowstorm, 116–120
Soldiers, 31
Spaugh, Addison, 160
Spaugh, Curtis, 13, 56, 65, 66, 67, 155, 156, 199
Speckled pup, 198
Spring water for drinking, 93
Sproul, Al, 173–177, 180
Stampede, 94, 95
Stetson hat, 150
Storey, John, 35, 136, 150, 154
Swan Land and Cattle Company, 11, 14
Swatky, Colonel, 110
Sybille Ditch, 1, 9

Texas, 25, 76, 114, 122, 123, 124, 126, 198
Thomas, J.B. (General manager of AU7), 96–97, 100, 101, 104, 105, 148, 199
Thorp, Russell, 13
Tobacco, 8, 26, 66, 88, 89, 90, 96, 105, 117, 203
TOT Ranch, 98
Town herd, 47–50
Tuckerman, Sol, 197

21 Ranch, 173, 175, 192
Tuff, Jimmy, 50, 52, 197, 199

ULA Ranch, 36–38, 39, 115
Union Pacific Railroad, 1, 3, 24

Valentine, Nebraska, 101
Van Tassel Ranch, 160, 164
Vermont, 63, 199
Visalia saddle, 179, 192, 206

Wages (for cowboys), 28, 29, 67, 80, 92, 135, 166, 206

Warren, Francis E., 13
Washing clothing, 39
Wellman, George, 171
West, Billy, 137, 140
What Cheer, Iowa, 25, 153
Whipping with chaps, 110
Whiskey, 5, 6, 90
Whitcomb, E.W., 13
Wild Bill, 111
Williams, J.T., 13, 197
Wyoming Stock Growers Association, 2, 26, 27, 28, 77–78, 79, 81